With Best Compliments From

Sikh Gurdwara San Jose
2785 Quimby Road, San Jose, CA 95148

Style of the Lion: The Sikhs*
Prologue
A glimpse into the *whys* and *hows* of the Sikh style

As humans we seek happiness through four paths. The first path is through our senses: healthful food, exercise, music, physical pleasure...also, drugs, self-mutilation, and gluttony.

The second involves our intellect: reading and writing books, solving complex problems...also, pursuing ideas to denigrate others.

Fame and fortune in society encompass the third path: nursing the sick and poor, educating others, preserving the environment...also, creating conflict in the name of race, skin color or gender.

These first three paths are the paths of duality—the world is separated into *me* and *you*. There is a fourth path where the *me-you* separateness disappears. Here, the individual is in resonance with the workings of the Creator. This path produces everlasting bliss.

How does one balance one's life among these four paths? God—Vaheguru (Wondrous Guru) for the Sikh—is Truth (Satnam) itself. The Sikh above all should be a seeker of Truth—not a follower of mere dogma. This book provides a glimpse of the Sikh view. Although the imagery used in this book is primarily of the male, the Sikh style has equal validity for men *and* for women.

* Sikh derived from Shishya (Sanskrit: Student)

STYLE OF THE LION: THE SIKHS

Jasprit Singh
design by Teresa Singh

STYLE OF THE LION: THE SIKHS

For more information, contact:

Akal Publications
P.O. Box 130563
Ann Arbor, MI 48113-0563
U.S.A.
email: singh@caen.engin.umich.edu

ISBN 0-9660942-0-4

Printed in the United States of America by E & G Printing Service, Inc., Madison Heights, Michigan.

Table of Contents

Style of the Lion: The Sikhs

Preface

Ever since I can remember, my father used to take me for morning walks in the beautiful lawns of India Gate in New Delhi. At five in the morning he would massage my legs with mustard oil ("you will not feel the cold," he claimed) and we would head off. On these walks he would answer the million logical and mostly illogical questions of a child. When he was not answering my questions, he would sing a *shabad* from the *Guru Granth Sahib*. Sometimes he would explain it to me. As I grew older he would apply the explanation to a problem I was facing. I believe now that these walks with my father provided the most important schooling in my life. On page seventy-three of this book I have reproduced — twenty-five years after it was told by my father to his nineteen year old son — a story that is central to the Sikh style.

Over the years I have felt a strong yearning to capture the Sikh style in a book and share it with Sikhs and non-Sikhs. This book is a first volume in this effort — focusing on the Sikh male style.

Guru Gobind Singh has given the Sikh a highly visual physical style. The turban, the acceptance of the Creator's gift of hair (*kesh*), makes the Sikh individual a colorful subject. This book is intended to be highly visual and concise.

I dedicate this book to my father, Giani Gurcharan Singh. And to my mother, Sardarni Gursharan Kaur. At the young age of seventy-seven, my mother coordinated all of the interviews for the book and trudged along on the photography sessions needed for this work.

Without the artistry and computer graphics skills of my wife, Teresa, this book would not have been possible.

I hope you enjoy this book. And remember that nothing is more welcome than a postcard or a letter giving us your feedback.

Jasprit Singh
singh@caen.engin.umich.edu

Akal Publications
P.O. Box 130563
Ann Arbor, MI 48113-0563
U.S.A.
www.akalsangat.com

Acknowledgements

We gratefully acknowledge discussions and insights provided by our numerous friends while developing ideas for this book. We are particularly grateful to the following people:

Lt. General Jagjit Singh Aurora,

Major Hari Pal Singh Ahluwalia,

Captain Man Mohan Singh Kohli,

Brigadier Surrinder Singh Nakai,

Sardar Gurbhagat Singh Gill,

Sardar Mewa Singh Sangha,

Sardar Piara Singh Data,

Sardar Rominder Singh Sangha,

Sardar Rajbir Singh for providing us half a dozen photographs used in this book,

The Anglo-Sikh War Memorial Museum of Ferozepur,

Professor Pashaura Singh for providing us precious feedback,

Lt. Colonel Moti Kataria and the Sikh soldiers, Havildar Bakhshish Singh and Sepoy Joga Singh, of the Sikh Regiment for permitting us to photograph in their center,

Yogi Harbhajan Singh and his associates at Guru Ram Das Ashram in Santa Monica for allowing us to photograph their worship,

our son, Nirala, for his illustrations,

and to our parents for their support and encouragement.

A Historical Perspective

A physical scientist serves two purposes by studying our physical universe — he or she can tell us how to harness physical forces for our good, and what ideas and actions are futile. By knowing what is futile, we can avoid being exploited by quacks and con artists.

The Sikh Gurus are the spiritual scientists who gave humanity two messages — what is the path that leads to spiritual bliss and what are rituals which are futile or even harmful.

By pointing out the futility of many rituals the Sikh Gurus have provided us a unique, crystal clear path towards bliss. This path is unfettered by side-tracking rituals concocted to please an "angry God;" it does not create superior and inferior beings through birth into the "right" or "wrong" caste; it does not make spiritual bliss the sole domain of men alone, keeping the women out; it does not advocate a family-less life in order to reach bliss; on the contrary, in the ups and downs of family life is bliss to be found.

An examination of the lives of humankind's great philosophers and religious founders reveals an interesting fact. Most of these men had little to do with women, or children, or the founding of businesses, or the joy of maintaining a good physique. The Sikh Gurus espoused and practiced philosophies while participating fully in society. They were superb horsemen, swordsmen, family men, and they established businesses and founded cities. Participation, not withdrawal, is the message. But the participation is not that of a glutton — it is that of a person under the Creator's grace.

Who were these visionary Gurus who gave such a message to the world? The Sikh philosophy is based upon the teachings of ten Gurus. The Guru for the Sikh is now *Sri Guru Granth Sahib* — an embodiment of the Gurus teachings along with passages from many other enlightened souls.

Guru Nanak (1469-1539)

Guru Nanak was the founder of the Sikh faith. Born during a time of great conflict between Hinduism and Islam, he had the broad vision to see how far these great religions had strayed from their once intended path. He saw Hinduism straying from its essence, sinking into mindless rituals and the utterly degrading caste system. He saw Islam deviating from its real message, becoming rigid and bent on conversion by sword, intolerant of any other interpretation of the infinite God.

Guru Angad (1504-1552)

Guru Nanak chose Guru Angad to succeed him, bypassing his own children. The second Guru, through example, inculcated in the Sikh the importance of humility, service to humanity, love of sportsmanship and acceptance of God's wonderful drama. He is said to have used *Gurmukhi*, the script of the *Guru Granth Sahib*, to introduce the Sikh philosophy to the common man. By rejecting the language of Sanskrit — a language only understood by priests — he dealt a severe blow to the priests of the time. His wife, Khivi, served the Sikh community along with Guru Angad.

Guru Amar Das (1479-1574)

Guru Amar Das was a disciple of Guru Angad and was chosen to carry the light of Guru Nanak. He made the *langar*, community kitchen, a central part of the Sikh social style. He also fought against *purdah* (the veil used by Muslim women) and *sati* (the perverse Hindu custom of forcing the widow to burn herself on her husband's funeral pyre). He compiled the teachings of the first two Gurus into four volumes, two of which are still extant. This compilation was an important source for the *Guru Granth Sahib*.

Guru Ram Das (1534-1581)

Guru Ram Das, the fourth Guru, was married to the daughter of Guru Amar Das. Believing in the importance of secular activities, he utilized his talents to establish cities and he founded *Ramdaspur*, now known as Amritsar. He encouraged Sikhs to get involved in trade advocating compatibility among the seemingly disparate aspects of household, business and spirituality.

Guru Arjun (1563-1606)

Guru Arjun was the youngest son of Guru Ram Das. A poet, builder and great organizer, Guru Arjun was also the first martyr in Sikh history. He built, in the heart of Amritsar, a *Gurdwara*, now commonly known as the Golden Temple. Open on all four sides, the temple signifies openness to men and women of all castes and from all corners of the world. Sain Mian Mir, a Muslim saint, was asked by the Guru to lay the foundation of this *Gurdwara*. Guru Arjun also built the cities of Taran Taran and Kartarpur.

Fearful of the Guru's influence upon Hindus and Muslims, the Mughal Emperor Jahangir ordered the arrest of the Guru. Guru Arjun was tortured to death in Lahore.

Guru Hargobind (1595-1644)

The martyrdom of Guru Arjun transformed the Sikhs from a pacifist people to a people unafraid to raise the sword against injustices. The apparent change in the Sikh community was a response of vigorous faith to the event of the times. Guru Nanak himself had risked his life by condemning Emperor Babar's impositions.

Guru Hargobind was the first Guru to introduce the importance of awakening the inner warrior against injustice. He began the practice of wearing a kirpan or sword. Horsemanship, marksmanship, swordsmanship and hunting were an integral part of this Guru's life. Opposite the Golden Temple he built a place of congregation — the Akal Takht.

Guru Hargobind had several skirmishes with Emperor Jahangir's army, but the fitness and form of his soldiers saved the day.

Guru Har Rai (1630-1661)

Guru Har Rai confirmed the tradition of warrior and saint among the Sikhs. An extremely tender hearted person, he was a fine swordsman, but would not injure anyone.

Guru Har Krishan (1656-1664)

The eighth Guru was barely five years old when he became Guru. Even at this young age his intelligence and vision were highly developed. It was clear he was no ordinary child.

Guru Teg Bahadur (1621-1675)

Guru Teg Bahadur became the ninth Guru of the Sikhs when he was forty-four years old. He faced great intrigue against him from many powerful forces determined to control the Sikh faith. However, his leadership and fearless attitude prevailed. Initially denied entrance into the Golden Temple by his detractors, Guru Teg Bahadur built the city of Anandpur.

In his zeal to convert Hindus to Islam, Mughal Emperor Aurangzeb imposed terrible laws on non-Muslims. The Guru spoke out on behalf of the Hindus. He was arrested in Agra and brought to Delhi where he was beheaded.

Guru Gobind Singh (1666-1708)

Guru Gobind Singh, the tenth Guru, assumed the Guruship in times of great turbulence. This learned man was fluent in Hindi, Sanskrit, Persian and Gurmukhi. He instilled in the Sikhs the joy of valor and sacrifice. The unbounded optimism which marks the Sikh faith is, to a large extent, due to Guru Gobind Singh.

Guru Gobind Singh's teachings stirred the people of the land. Desire for freedom from corrupt landlords and kings was revived in people who, for centuries, had been indoctrinated to accept their lot and to sulk in their misery. This development caused both Hindu Rajas and the Muslim Emperor to launch attacks on the Guru.

On Baisakhi day (Spring festival) of 1699, at Anandpur, Guru Gobind Singh formed the Khalsa[1]. With a naked sword he asked for a human sacrifice — five times. One by one the volunteers were led away. However, they were not beheaded — they formed the *panj piaras* (the five loved ones). The Guru baptized them and in turn was baptized by them. Other Sikhs were also baptized — by sharing sugared water stirred with a double-edged sword— the ritual shedding of their castes. Guru Gobind Singh also gave the Sikhs the great privilege of wearing the five "k"'s (*kesh*, unshorn hair; *kangha*, a comb to keep the hair clean and tidy; *kara*, a steel bangle representing the omnipresence of God and resolve; *kachha*, or shorts, a symbol of chastity and labor; and *kirpan*, a sword for fighting injustice (both within and without).

Sri Guru Granth Sahib (timeless)

Sri Guru Granth Sahib — a compilation of the *shabads* (hymns) of the Sikh Gurus and many other Hindu and Muslim men of God — is now the Guru for all Sikhs. Each *shabad* — cast in the highest level of poetry — is assigned a musical measure from the Indian classical music system. The musical measures are chosen to neither excite nor cause a depressed mood. The purpose of the music is to create calmness of body and spirit — not a temporary state of excitement.

The *Dasam Granth* — a compilation of the writings of Guru Gobind Singh — also forms an important source of inspiration for the Sikh.

Note: In the following chapters, important concepts are discussed by drawing from *shabads* from the *Guru Granth Sahib* (GGS) and *Dasam Granth* (DG). An English form is also provided. We have not followed the standard scholarly rules of transliteration of Gurmukhi to English. This is a choice of convenience, biased towards the lay reader. We hope that readers with more scholarly background will not be distracted.

---

[1] *Khalsa represents purity of thought and action.*

The Sikh Style

ੴ ਸਤਿਨਾਮੁ ਕਰਤਾ ਪੁਰਖੁ ਨਿਰਭਉ ਨਿਰਵੈਰੁ
ਅਕਾਲ ਮੂਰਤਿ ਅਜੂਨੀ ਸੈਭੰ ਗੁਰ ਪ੍ਰਸਾਦਿ ॥

॥ ਜਪੁ ॥

ਆਦਿ ਸਚੁ ਜੁਗਾਦਿ ਸਚੁ ॥ ਹੈ ਭੀ ਸਚੁ ਨਾਨਕ ਹੋਸੀ ਭੀ ਸਚੁ ॥੧॥
ਸੋਚੈ ਸੋਚਿ ਨ ਹੋਵਈ ਜੇ ਸੋਚੀ ਲਖ ਵਾਰ ॥ ਚੁਪੈ ਚੁਪ ਨ ਹੋਵਈ ਜੇ ਲਾਇ ਰਹਾ ਲਿਵ ਤਾਰ ॥ ਭੁਖਿਆ ਭੁਖ ਨ ਉਤਰੀ ਜੇ ਬੰਨਾ ਪੁਰੀਆ ਭਾਰ ॥ ਸਹਸ ਸਿਆਣਪਾ ਲਖ ਹੋਹਿ ਤ ਇਕ ਨ ਚਲੈ ਨਾਲਿ ॥ ਕਿਵ ਸਚਿਆਰਾ ਹੋਈਐ ਕਿਵ ਕੂੜੈ ਤੁਟੈ ਪਾਲਿ ॥ ਹੁਕਮਿ ਰਜਾਈ ਚਲਣਾ ਨਾਨਕ ਲਿਖਿਆ ਨਾਲਿ ॥੧॥ ਹੁਕਮੀ ਹੋਵਨਿ ਆਕਾਰ ਹੁਕਮੁ ਨ ਕਹਿਆ ਜਾਈ ॥ ਹੁਕਮੀ ਹੋਵਨਿ ਜੀਅ ਹੁਕਮਿ ਮਿਲੈ ਵਡਿਆਈ ॥ ਹੁਕਮੀ ਉਤਮੁ ਨੀਚੁ ਹੁਕਮਿ ਲਿਖਿ ਦੁਖ ਸੁਖ ਪਾਈਅਹਿ ॥ ਇਕਨਾ ਹੁਕਮੀ ਬਖਸੀਸ ਇਕਿ ਹੁਕਮੀ ਸਦਾ ਭਵਾਈਅਹਿ ॥ ਹੁਕਮੈ ਅੰਦਰਿ ਸਭੁ ਕੋ ਬਾਹਰਿ ਹੁਕਮ ਨ ਕੋਇ ॥ ਨਾਨਕ ਹੁਕਮੈ ਜੇ ਬੁਝੈ ਤ ਹਉਮੈ ਕਹੈ ਨ ਕੋਇ ॥੨॥ ਗਾਵੈ ਕੋ ਤਾਣੁ ਹੋਵੈ ਕਿਸੈ ਤਾਣੁ ॥ ਗਾਵੈ ਕੋ ਦਾਤਿ ਜਾਣੈ ਨੀਸਾਣੁ ॥ ਗਾਵੈ ਕੋ ਗੁਣ ਵਡਿਆਈਆ ਚਾਰ ॥ ਗਾਵੈ ਕੋ ਵਿਦਿਆ ਵਿਖਮੁ ਵੀਚਾਰੁ ॥ ਗਾਵੈ ਕੋ ਸਾਜਿ ਕਰੇ ਤਨੁ ਖੇਹ ॥ ਗਾਵੈ ਕੋ ਜੀਅ ਲੈ ਫਿਰਿ ਦੇਹ ॥ ਗਾਵੈ ਕੋ ਜਾਪੈ ਦਿਸੈ

One Supreme Being. He is Truth. He is the Creator. Without Fear. Inimical to None. Beyond Time. Not Incarnated; Self-Created. The Enlightener. Realized by the Grace of the True Guru.

True in the beginning, True in the primeval age, True now and True for times to come. Thinking does not realize Him, no matter how hard one thinks; Neither does silence, no matter how much one withdraws. Man's hunger remains unsatiated, no matter what he gathers; his intellect may be immense, but it helps not in the journey. How then is the Truth revealed? How is the veil of untruth to be torn? Says Nanak, by accepting and following His laws. His laws have created all forms, though one knows not how. Through His command is life created; His laws bestow honor. Through His will is greatness, lowliness, sorrow, joy. Some blessed, some caught in the cycle (of joy and sorrow). All mortals are subject to these laws; none is beyond them. Nanak says, once the laws are revealed, "I," "Mine," departs. The Mighty sing of His might, the blessed of his boons; Some sing of His virtues, immense knowledge. Some sing of how He creates and annihilates; Some sing of how He takes life, then infuses it. Some sing of how far He is, Some see Him face-to-face,....

Guru Nanak (GGS p. 1)

Every religion and culture has its own style of leading one from birth to death. The Sikh style has been bestowed upon us by the ten *Gurus*. Many Sikhs have lived the Sikh style — often at great personal risk — and have influenced the Sikh style.

The style of the Sikh is not one concocted by thinkers sitting at river banks or in caves. It comes to us through men who have participated in life and surpassed the cycle of joy and sorrow.

Guru Nanak's divine *Shabads* come to us from one who traveled the world, participated in business, and raised a family; from one who treated the Emperor and the poor farmer with equal grace.

Guru Gobind Singh-ji's martial poetry emerges from one who has been in the fire of battles; from one whose two sons were bricked alive. This supreme poet has given the Sikhs the incomparable *Dasam Granth*.

The Sikh style for men (the *Singhs* or lions) is one which guides a child through the state of boyhood into the state of manhood and onto the final state of bliss.

A Universal Style

Let us take a look at one aspect of the Sikh style by entering one of the large *Gurdwaras* in a cosmopolitan city. You remove your shoes and hand them to a volunteer who dusts them and places them in a cubicle for you. You are surprised that a large number of these volunteers are Hindus or Muslims who find the simple beauty of Sikhism very attractive, even though by tradition they have allegiance to another religion.

You wash your feet and enter the main hall where the *Guru Granth Sahib* presides. As a *jatha*[1] sings a *shabad*[2] from the *Guru Granth Sahib*, you find men and women from all walks of life and from many different religions sitting and swaying.

These *Gurdwaras* do not just open their doors during specific *holy* times — they are open for all at any time. *All times are appropriate for meditation and for balancing your life*, even though most people prefer the calm of the early mornings.

What gives the Sikh religion its universality and eternal appeal? It is the *Granth Sahib* — the Guru.

Balihari Guru aapne duiharhi sad var jin manas te devte kiye karat na lagi var.

Myriad times a day I am sacrificed to my Guru
who transforms men into divine beings and does so instantly.
Guru Nanak (GGS p. 162)

Je soh chanda ugave suraj charhe hazar ete chanan hodia Guru bin ghor andhar.

A hundred moons may blossom, a thousand suns may blaze,
in this intense brightness, without my Guru there is pitch darkness.
Guru Angad (GGS p. 463)

[1] A jatha is a group of three or four singers.
[2] A shabad is a hymn.

The Guru Granth Sahib: A Distilled Style

The *Guru Granth Sahib* is the living Guru for the Sikh. It is often said that the *Guru Granth Sahib* is like the Bible for Christians or the Koran for Muslims. However, there are key differences as well. While most great religions have similar answers to the question, "What should I do?" there are different answers to the question, "Why should I do it?" The Sikh Gurus have offered humanity divine wisdom, but have not fallen into the usual trap of trying to explain the intimate workings of the Creator — how can a finite human truly grasp the Infinite One?

The first paragraph of the *Guru Granth Sahib* is reproduced at the beginning of this chapter. It presents the essence of the Sikh belief.

The *Guru Granth Sahib* does not begin with an explanation of how God created the world, how He created man and woman, how woman caused the downfall of man, nor does it describe the intimate details of how God felt, or how angels and devils fought. There is no list of holy foods to eat; no prescribed holy times to pray; no mention of holy rivers to bathe in; no requirements of pilgrimages to make; nor any necessary rituals to purge the sins.

For the Sikh Gurus, attempts to explain the intimate behavior of our Creator are futile and distracting. By keeping legends and miracles out of the *Guru Granth Sahib*, the Gurus have blessed the Sikhs. The Sikh is not burdened by perpetual debates on unprovable assertions — instead he or she can focus on the central issues of creating *anand*[1] in his or her life. The Sikh Gurus have often referred to the great Indian mythologies to make important concepts clear. The *Granth Sahib* contains works of many Islamic divine men as well. This has brought to the Sikhs important concepts from the great Western philosophies. However, the Gurus have been quite clear in assuring the Sikh that legends and myths are tools to learn valuable concepts — not to be taken as literal teachings of the Creator's laws.

Religious legends and mythologies are useful attempts to teach universal concepts. However, they are also abused to divide man against man and to create fervor among the devout in order to kill and destroy.

When the Spanish came to the Americas (by mistake) they found a rich society with enormous wealth. Once they learned that they were not in India, they wondered how they could exploit the New World. An answer came from the Church's interpretation of the Bible. The Church scholars decided that since there was no mention of these new tribes in the Bible, then these people had no soul; therefore, it was morally justified to take their wealth by any means. This *divine* interpretation gave the Spaniards the moral upper hand. The Natives were butchered and their wealth plundered. Of course, it is unimaginable that Jesus Christ could have ever intended his followers to go on this path. It took fifty years for the Church to declare that they had erred!

The most unfortunate outcome of the literal interpretation of religious legends has been the slaughter of the Jews by Germans. Hitler's hatred of Jews (and of many other non-Germans) was encouraged by the Church of the land which seriously believed that since Jesus Christ was crucified by Jews, the Jewish people were cursed by God. Fortunately, now the

---

[1] *Anand means bliss.*

Church has altered its position.

The history of mankind is full of periods where religious legends have been exploited to create the energy needed to decimate other people.

Even though the Sikh Gurus themselves suffered greatly at the hands of the Muslim rulers as well as the Hindu Rajas of the time, the *Guru Granth Sahib* is remarkably devoid of these conflicts. The Gurus gave us a distilled eternal Guru in the *Guru Granth Sahib*.

ਤੂ ਦਰੀਆਉ ਦਾਨਾ ਬੀਨਾ ਮੈ ਮਛੁਲੀ ਕੈਸੇ ਅੰਤੁ ਲਹਾ ॥
ਜਹ ਜਹ ਦੇਖਾ ਤਹ ਤਹ ਤੂ ਹੈ ਤੁਝ ਤੇ ਨਿਕਸੀ ਫੂਟਿ ਮਰਾ ॥੧॥

Toon dariyao dana bina main machhli kaise ant laha.
Jah jah dekha tah tah Tu hai, Tujh se niksi phoot mara.

You, a limitless sea, I, a fish; how can I describe You?
Wherever I see, You reside; I shrivel away without You.
Guru Nanak (GGS p. 25)

ਚੱਕ੍ਰ ਚਿਹਨ ਅਰੁ ਬਰਨ ਜਾਤਿ ਅਰੁ ਪਾਤਿ ਨਹਿਨ ਜਿਹ ॥ ਰੂਪ ਰੰਗ ਅਰੁ ਰੇਖ ਭੇਖ ਕੋਊ ਕਹਿ ਨ ਸਕਤਿ ਕਿਹ ॥
ਅਚਲ ਮੂਰਤਿ ਅਨਭਉ ਪ੍ਰਕਾਸ਼ ਅਮਿਤੋਜ ਕਹਿੱਜੈ ॥ ਕੋਟਿ ਇੰਦ੍ਰ ਇੰਦ੍ਰਾਣਿ ਸਾਹਿ ਸਾਹਾਣਿ ਗਨਿੱਜੈ ॥
ਤ੍ਰਿਭਵਣ ਮਹੀਪ ਸੁਰ ਨਰ ਅਸੁਰ ਨੇਤਿ ਨੇਤਿ ਬਨ ਤ੍ਰਿਨ ਕਹਤ ॥ ਤਵ ਸਰਬ ਨਾਮ ਕੱਥੈ ਕਵਨ ਕਰਮ ਨਾਮ ਬਰਨਤ ਸੁਮਤਿ ॥

Chakr chihan ar baran jat ar pat nahin jeh.
Rup rang ar rekh bekh kau kah na sakat keh.
Achal murat anbhau prakas amitoj kahijai.
Kot indr indran sah sahan ganijai.
Tribhavan mahip sur nar asur, net net ban trin kahat.
Tar sarab Nam kathai karan, karam Nam barnat sumat.

The creator has no halo, no special marks, no color, no caste, no lineage.
None can describe his form, complexion, outline or dress.
He is perpetual, self-illuminated, and has limitless power.
He is Lord of countless Indras and King of all Kings.
He is the Emperor of the three worlds; demigods, men, demons.
Woods and pastures proclaim you indestructible.
Such is Your virtue that no one name can describe you.
Wise men choose a Name appropriate to your Excellence.
Guru Gobind Singh (DG p. 1)

The Sikh View of the Universe We Live In

The self-existent Creator has endowed our universe with His *hukams*, or laws. The entire universe operates within these laws. No one is beyond these laws. There are scientific laws which govern our physical universe — they tell us how the earth spins and moves around the sun. But there are laws in which our mind is an active participant. These are the laws that allow us to view great tragedies as challenges; to treat the mighty emperor and the poor peasant with equal respect; to expand beyond our ego and to feel one with the entire universe thus reaching the state of bliss.

The scientist deals with the physical laws of our universe. These laws create magical technologies, wonder drugs to treat our illnesses and even promise entirely new kinds of life forms, thanks to genetic technologies.

The scientist bases his or her creations on one very important truth — *the laws are applicable at all times and in all places*. No scientist would design an aircraft assuming that during some special times determined by holy men the earth will not pull the plane down!

Understanding and following the laws of physics allow us to build airplanes that fly faster than the speed of sound, computers that compute at blinding speeds and other technological marvels. In our own daily life we are aware of these laws — often subconsciously. If we ignore the laws of gravity, we stumble and fall.

The *Guru Granth Sahib* tells us that following the spiritual laws — *hukams* — leads to an escape from the joy-sorrow cycle. This path does not involve ego-stroking rituals like pilgrimages, fasting, deprivations of the body's needs, or body mutilations. These rituals are irrelevant and often harmful. The path involves overcoming one's *haumai* — self-centered approach to life — and to feel as one with the entire Creation. It involves developing a healthy body, mind and spirit. On this path a man does not run from society — he participates and contributes while still achieving this high spiritual state. He is an involved warrior — a saint-warrior. The person who lives his or her life in these *hukams* has absorbed *Nam* — has understood the essence of bliss.

ਸਲੋਕ ਮਃ ੧ ॥

ਭੈ ਵਿਚਿ ਪਵਣੁ ਵਹੈ ਸਦਵਾਉ ॥ ਭੈ ਵਿਚਿ ਚਲਹਿ ਲਖ ਦਰੀਆਉ ॥ ਭੈ ਵਿਚਿ ਅਗਨਿ ਕਢੈ ਵੇਗਾਰਿ ॥
ਭੈ ਵਿਚਿ ਧਰਤੀ ਦਬੀ ਭਾਰਿ ॥ ਭੈ ਵਿਚਿ ਇੰਦੁ ਫਿਰੈ ਸਿਰ ਭਾਰਿ ॥ ਭੈ ਵਿਚਿ ਰਾਜਾ ਧਰਮ ਦੁਆਰੁ ॥
ਭੈ ਵਿਚਿ ਸੂਰਜੁ ਭੈ ਵਿਚਿ ਚੰਦੁ ॥ ਕੋਹ ਕਰੋੜੀ ਚਲਤ ਨ ਅੰਤੁ ॥ ਭੈ ਵਿਚਿ ਸਿਧ ਬੁਧ ਸੁਰ ਨਾਥ ॥
ਭੈ ਵਿਚਿ ਆਡਾਣੇ ਆਕਾਸ ॥ ਭੈ ਵਿਚਿ ਜੋਧ ਮਹਾਬਲ ਸੂਰ ॥ ਭੈ ਵਿਚਿ ਆਵਹਿ ਜਾਵਹਿ ਪੂਰ ॥
ਸਗਲਿਆ ਭਉ ਲਿਖਿਆ ਸਿਰਿ ਲੇਖੁ ॥ ਨਾਨਕ ਨਿਰਭਉ ਨਿਰੰਕਾਰੁ ਸਚੁ ਏਕੁ ॥ ੧ ॥

Bhai[1] vich pawan vahai sadvao.

Bhai vich chalah lakh dariao.

Bhai vich agan(i) kadai vagar(i).

Bhai vich dharti dabi bhar(i).

Bhai vich ind(u) phirai sir bhar(i) Bhai vich raja dharam duar.

Bhai vich suraj bhai vich chand.

Koh crorhi chalat na ant.

Bhai vich sidh budh sur nath.

Bhai vich adane akas.

Bhai vich jodh mahabal sur.

Bhai vich are jave pur.

Sagalia bhau likhia sir lekh.

Nanak nirbhau nirankar sach ek.

Within His laws blows the wind with its myriad breezes.
Within His laws flow a myriad of rivers.
Within His laws does the fire labor.
Within His laws does Earth bear its burden.
Within His laws do the clouds move headlong.
Within His laws Dharam Raj[2] sits at Lord's gate.
Within His laws blazes the sun, shines the moon.
Also moves aeons of time, and miles without end.
Within His laws are the Sidhas, Buddhas, and Naths[3].
Within His laws does the sky stretch endlessly.
Within His laws enter and depart humans.
His command reigns above all.
Nanak says, beyond laws is the One, Formless, True Lord.

Guru Nanak (GGS p. 464)

[1] *Bhai translates as fear.*
[2] *Dharam Raj is the mythological "tally man" of good and bad deeds performed in one's life.*
[3] *Sidhas, Buddhas and Naths are various categories of Holy Men.*

Ego Stroking Rituals

The *Guru Granth Sahib* begins by describing the futility of performing myriads of rituals in order to achieve bliss. Yet when most people talk of a religious experience it is precisely these rituals that are discussed.

Pilgrimages, discussions of how God built this universe, how He breaks His own rules through miracles, how He can be pleased by taking baths in holy rivers, etc., are only designed to stroke the ego. These rituals only serve to create rifts between men and to take one away from the central issues of spirituality.

ਹਉਮੈ ਏਹਾ ਜਾਤਿ ਹੈ ਹਉਮੈ ਕਰਮ ਕਮਾਹਿ ॥ ਹਉਮੈ ਏਈ ਬੰਧਨਾ ਫਿਰਿ ਫਿਰਿ ਜੋਨੀ ਪਾਹਿ ॥
ਹਉਮੈ ਕਿਥਹੁ ਊਪਜੈ ਕਿਤੁ ਸੰਜਮਿ ਇਹ ਜਾਇ ॥ ਹਉਮੈ ਏਹੋ ਹੁਕਮੁ ਹੈ ਪਇਐ ਕਿਰਤਿ ਫਿਰਾਹਿ ॥
ਹਉਮੈ ਦੀਰਘ ਰੋਗੁ ਹੈ ਦਾਰੂ ਭੀ ਇਸੁ ਮਾਹਿ ॥ ਕਿਰਪਾ ਕਰੇ ਜੇ ਆਪਣੀ ਤਾ ਗੁਰ ਕਾ ਸਬਦੁ ਕਮਾਹਿ ॥
ਨਾਨਕੁ ਕਹੈ ਸੁਣਹੁ ਜਨਹੁ ਇਤੁ ਸੰਜਮਿ ਦੁਖ ਜਾਹਿ ॥

Haumai ehaa jaat(i) hai haumai karam kamahi.
Haumai eii bandhana phir phir joonii rahi.
Haumai kitthu oopjai kit sanjam eh jaai.
Haumai ehoo hukam hai paiai kirat phirahi.
Haumai diragh roog hai diiroo bhii is mahi.
Kirpaa karee je aapnii taa Gur kaa sabad kamahi.
Nanak kahai sunahu janahu itu sanjam dukh jahi.

Such is the nature of ego that we act within ego.
Such is egos bondage that we revolve in this cycle.
How does ego evolve? How does it depart?
Ego is His Creation, we receive it and act in it.
Ego is a chronic malady, but within it also lies the medicine.
When His grace is bestowed, His divine laws are observed.
Nanak says: Hear O folks, this practice causes sorrow to depart.

Guru Angad (GGS p. 466)

16

ਲਿਖਿ ਲਿਖਿ ਪੜਿਆ ॥ ਤੇਤਾ ਕੜਿਆ ॥ ਬਹੁ ਤੀਰਥ ਭਵਿਆ ॥ ਤੇਤੋ ਲਵਿਆ ॥ ਬਹੁ ਭੇਖ ਕੀਆ ਦੇਹੀ ਦੁਖੁ ਦੀਆ ॥
ਸਹੁ ਵੇ ਜੀਆ ਅਪਣਾ ਕੀਆ ॥ ਅੰਨੁ ਨ ਖਾਇਆ ਸਾਦੁ ਗਵਾਇਆ ॥ ਬਹੁ ਦੁਖੁ ਪਾਇਆ ਦੂਜਾ ਭਾਇਆ ॥
ਬਸਤ੍ਰੁ ਨ ਪਹਿਰੈ ॥ ਅਹਿਨਿਸਿ ਕਹਰੈ ॥ ਮੋਨਿ ਵਿਗੂਤਾ ॥ ਕਿਉ ਜਾਗੈ ਗੁਰ ਬਿਨੁ ਸੂਤਾ ॥ ਪਗ ਉਪੇਤਾਣਾ ॥
ਅਪਣਾ ਕੀਆ ਕਮਾਣਾ ॥ ਅਲੁ ਮਲੁ ਖਾਈ ਸਿਰਿ ਛਾਈ ਪਾਈ ॥ ਮੂਰਖਿ ਅੰਧੈ ਪਤਿ ਗਵਾਈ ॥
ਵਿਣੁ ਨਾਵੈ ਕਿਛੁ ਥਾਇ ਨ ਪਾਈ ॥ ਰਹੈ ਬੇਬਾਣੀ ਮੜੀ ਮਸਾਣੀ ॥ ਅੰਧੁ ਨ ਜਾਣੈ ਫਿਰਿ ਪਛੁਤਾਣੀ ॥
ਸਤਿਗੁਰੁ ਭੇਟੇ ਸੋ ਸੁਖੁ ਪਾਏ ॥ ਹਰਿ ਕਾ ਨਾਮੁ ਮੰਨਿ ਵਸਾਏ ॥ ਨਾਨਕ ਨਦਰਿ ਕਰੇ ਸੋ ਪਾਏ ॥
ਆਸ ਅੰਦੇਸੇ ਤੇ ਨਿਹਕੇਵਲੁ ਹਉਮੈ ਸਬਦਿ ਜਲਾਏ ॥

Likh likh parhiah. Teta khariah.
Bahoo tirath bhaviah. Tete lavia.
Bahu bhekh kia dehi dukh dia. Sahu ve jiia apna kiia.
An na khaia saad gavaaia. Bahu dukh paiaa doojaa bhaaia.
Bastra na pahire. Ahinis(i) kahrai.
Mon vigootaa. Kau jage Gur bin suta.
Pag oopetanaa. Apnaa kiia kamaanaa.
Al mal khaaii, sir chaaii paaii. Murakh andhee pat gavaaii.
Bin naavai kich thai na paaii.
Kahai bebanii marhii masaanii. Andh na janai phir pachtaani.
Satgur(u) bhete so sukh pac. Har ka nuum man vasae.
Nanak nadar kare so paae. Aas andese te nikhval haumai Sabad jalae.

More and more he reads and writes; torments surround him.
More pilgrimages he organizes; these bring more prattles.
More robes he changes; his body suffers. All these sufferings; it is his own doing.
He gives up food; loses his taste. He craves <u>maya</u>; receives sorrow.
Gives up clothing; groans night and day; sinks into silence.
How can he be awakened without the Guru?
Goes around barefoot; suffers due to his own deeds.
Eats filth; throws ashes on his head. A blind fool; he loses his dignity.
Without <u>Nam</u> he finds no resting place; he lives in wilderness and in cemeteries.
Blind, ignorant of the essence, he repents in the end.
Only he who meets the True Guru finds peace.
For he absorbs his path (Nam) in his heart.
Nanak: His grace provides this gift.
Hope and despair vanish. His ego is burnt off by His word.
Guru Nanak (GGS p. 467)

Expanding Our Existence

Anyone who has observed small children can see how they progress through various stages of development. A two-year old clings to his toys with the words, "mine, mine, mine." As he grows a little older he learns the benefits of sharing his toys with his friends. He sees that by sharing he can not only have access to other toys, but he can play games which he cannot play by himself. If the child continues to develop in a healthy environment, he becomes a valuable citizen of the world. If he does not develop in a healthy manner, he experiences a lifetime of poor relations with others. His self-focused approach not only gives him misery, but it also creates sorrow for those with whom he comes into contact.

How can a human being overcome *haumai*? The Creator has made such wondrous laws that a human can reach heights of greatness as well as depths of depravation. He can be a great healer or a murderer.

The process of expanding our being from a self-focused lifestyle to a universal style is a difficult one, especially in view of the many distractions present which promise fun and joy if we have a selfish style. It involves acceptance that we are a part of the entire universe and a life based on this principle will lead to bliss. This is what the *Guru Granth Sahib* promises us.

The process of becoming a Universal being benefits us by bringing health to us, our family and to anyone who comes in contact with us. Such a Universal being is not a slave to other people's power.

ਹਉ ਵਿਚਿ ਆਇਆ ਹਉ ਵਿਚਿ ਗਇਆ ॥ ਹਉ ਵਿਚਿ ਜੰਮਿਆ ਹਉ ਵਿਚਿ ਮੂਆ ॥
ਹਉ ਵਿਚਿ ਦਿਤਾ ਹਉ ਵਿਚਿ ਲਇਆ ॥ ਹਉ ਵਿਚਿ ਖਟਿਆ ਹਉ ਵਿਚਿ ਗਇਆ ॥
ਹਉ ਵਿਚਿ ਸਚਿਆਰੁ ਕੁੜਿਆਰੁ ॥ ਹਉ ਵਿਚਿ ਪਾਪ ਪੁੰਨ ਵੀਚਾਰੁ ॥ ਹਉ ਵਿਚਿ ਨਰਕਿ ਸੁਰਗਿ ਅਵਤਾਰੁ ॥
ਹਉ ਵਿਚਿ ਹਸੈ ਹਉ ਵਿਚਿ ਰੋਵੈ ॥ ਹਉ ਵਿਚਿ ਭਰੀਐ ਹਉ ਵਿਚਿ ਧੋਵੈ ॥ ਹਉ ਵਿਚਿ ਜਾਤੀ ਜਿਨਸੀ ਖੋਵੈ ॥
ਹਉ ਵਿਚਿ ਮੂਰਖੁ ਹਉ ਵਿਚਿ ਸਿਆਣਾ ॥ ਮੋਖ ਮੁਕਤਿ ਕੀ ਸਾਰ ਨ ਜਾਣਾ ॥
ਹਉ ਵਿਚਿ ਮਾਇਆ ਹਉ ਵਿਚਿ ਛਾਇਆ ॥ ਹਉਮੈ ਕਰਿ ਕਰਿ ਜੰਤ ਉਪਾਇਆ ॥ ਹਉਮੈ ਬੂਝੈ ਤਾ ਦਰੁ ਸੂਝੈ ॥
ਗਿਆਨ ਵਿਹੂਣਾ ਕਥਿ ਕਥਿ ਲੂਝੈ ॥ ਨਾਨਕ ਹੁਕਮੀ ਲਿਖੀਐ ਲੇਖੁ ॥ ਜੇਹਾ ਵੇਖਹਿ ਤੇਹਾ ਵੇਖੁ ॥

Haoo vich aavaa haoo vich gaiaa. Haoo vich janmiaa haoo vich muaa.
Haoo vich ditaa haoo vich laiaa. Haoo vich khatiaa haoo vich gaiaa.
Haoo vich sachiaar kuhiaar. Haoo vich paap pun vichaar.
Haoo vich narak surag avtaar.
Haoo vich hasai haoo vich rovai. Haoo vich bharia haoo vich dhovai.
Haoo vich jaatii jinsii khovai. Haoou vich moorakh hau vich siaanaa.
Mookh mukat ki saar naa jaanaa. Haoo vich maiaa haoo vich chaiaa.
Haumai kar(i) kar(i) jant upaaiaa. Haumai bujhai taa dar soojhai.
Gian vihoonaa kath kath loojhai.
Nanak hukmii likhiai lekh. Jehaa vekhah teha vekhu.

In ego one comes, in ego does one depart. In ego is one born, in ego does one die.
In ego one gives, in ego does one receive. In ego one earns, in ego does one waste.
In ego is one truthful and also a liar. In ego come thoughts of virtue and of sins.
In ego one lands in heaven or in hell. In ego does he laugh, in ego, cry.
In ego he sins, in ego does he absolve his sins.
In ego he loses the distinction of caste and creed. In ego is he foolish, in ego wise.
In ego one knows not the essence of deliverence.
In ego is one caught in the web of maya, in ego are shadows of doubt.
In ego is one caught in the cycle.
When he resoves the I-am-ness, he sees the doors open.
Without wisdom he prattles and debates.
Nanak says his laws govern our destiny. As sees He, so should we.
Guru Nanak (GGS p. 466)

A Complete Self

To reach the state of universal being one has to start with the self and reach a healthy state where there is good balance of one's own physical, mental and spiritual faculties. The Sikh lifestyle is strongly influenced by the saint-poet-warrior Guru Gobind Singh who has shown the world that it is indeed possible to reach such a balance. He has shown through his own life that you do not have to abandon your physical well-being to reach spiritual heights, or your mental well-being to become a man of God.

The importance of physical well-being can be judged from Guru Gobind Singh's *Dasam Granth*. The importance of valor and the role of the warrior is central to the Sikh style. The Sikh cannot be a glutton or a jungle-bound ascetic. He must *participate* in the world.

ਦੇਹੁਰਾ ਮਸੀਤ ਸੋਈ ਪੂਜਾ ਔ ਨਿਵਾਜ ਓਇ ਮਾਨਸ ਸਭੈ ਏਕ ਪੈ ਅਨੇਕ ਕੋ ਭੁਮਾਉ ਹੈ॥
ਦੇਵਤਾ ਅਦੇਵ ਜੱਛ ਗੰਧ੍ਰਬ ਤੁਰਕ ਹਿੰਦੂ ਨਜਾਰੇ ਨਜਾਰੇ ਦੇਸਨ ਕੇ ਭੇਸ ਕੋ ਪ੍ਰਭਾਉ ਹੈ॥
ਏਕੈ ਨੈਨ ਏਕੈ ਕਾਨ ਏਕੈ ਦੇਹ ਏਕੈ ਬਾਨ ਖਾਕ ਬਾਦ ਆਤਸ਼ ਔ ਆਬ ਕੋ ਰਲਾਉ ਹੈ॥
ਅਲਹ ਅਭੇਖ ਸੋਈ ਪੁਰਾਨ ਔ ਕੁਰਾਨ ਓਈ ਏਕ ਹੀ ਸਰੂਪ ਸਭੈ ਏਕ ਹੀ ਬਨਾਉ ਹੈ॥

Dehra masit soi puja aa nivaj oi manas sabhai ek pai anek ko bhramau hai.
Devata adev jach gandharbh turak hindu nayare nayare desan ke bhes ko prabhau hai.
Ekai nain ekai kan ekai deh ekai ban khak bad aatash aa aab ko katau hai.
Alah abhekh soi puran aa kuran oi ek hi sarup sabhai ek hi banau hai.

He is in the temple and the mosque. In the Hindu's pooja and the Muslim's namaz.
All humans have one origin though they appear different.
Deities, demons, divine musicians, Hindus, and Muslims are all His,
though regional dresses appear to create a distinction.
The same eyes, same ears, same physique, same figure,
all from earth, air, fire and water.
The Formless One (of Hindus) and Allah (of Muslims) are one;
the Koran and Puran praise Him. All have the same form made by Him.
Guru Gobind Singh (DG, p. 19)

From Self to Householder

The Sikh lifestyle is influenced by the remarkable fact that each of the Sikh Gurus who reached marriageable age established a household and had a family. They had businesses which they managed and were involved with the difficult tasks of raising children.

The importance of the householder's path cannot be overemphasized in the Sikh style. This is the ultimate test by fire for a man. The family allows a man's *lofty theoretical ideas* to be tested in real life. These lofty ideas are rapidly attacked by the children of the family. The family brings the man who, by nature, prefers to float on imaginary clouds down to earth. His imaginary forts are smashed, his incredible strength is shown to be phony.

At the dawn of the twenty-first century, the most powerful country in the world is the United States of America. Fifty percent of the marriages in the United States end in divorce. And increasingly, men do not want to be around children. Men who have built multi-billion dollar industries, who have shown incredible valor in the battlefield, who have fought and won bitter political battles have found that they are unable to survive in their own families. They cannot deal with being constantly forced to stay on the ground rather than floating in the clouds.

Indeed, nowhere is the need for expanding your ego beyond yourself more important than in the family.

ਸਚਿ ਸਿਮਰਿਐ ਹੋਵੈ ਪਰਗਾਸੁ ॥ ਤਾ ਤੇ ਬਿਖਿਆ ਮਹਿ ਰਹੈ ਉਦਾਸੁ ॥
ਸਤਿਗੁਰ ਕੀ ਐਸੀ ਵਡਿਆਈ ॥ ਪੁਤ੍ਰ ਕਲਤ੍ਰ ਵਿਚੇ ਗਤਿ ਪਾਈ ॥ ੨ ॥
ਐਸੀ ਸੇਵਕੁ ਸੇਵਾ ਕਰੈ ॥ ਜਿਸ ਕਾ ਜੀਉ ਤਿਸੁ ਆਗੈ ਧਰੈ ॥
ਸਾਹਿਬ ਭਾਵੈ ਸੋ ਪਰਵਾਨੁ ॥ ਸੋ ਸੇਵਕੁ ਦਰਗਹ ਪਾਵੈ ਮਾਨੁ ॥

Sach(i) simrio hovai pargaas. Taa te bikhiaa mahi rahai udaas.
Satgur kii aaisii vaddiaii. Putra kalatra viche gat(i) paaii.
Aisii sevak sevaa karai. Jis kaa jiio tis aagai dharai.
Sahib bhavai so parvan. So sevak dargah pavai maan.

He who meditates on the Truth, shall be illumined. In <u>maya</u> he will remain detached.
Such is the True Guru's glory; in the midst of the household is one emancipated.
Such service the Lord's servant renders; his life to Him he surrenders.
He accepts His command, and in His court he receives glory.

Guru Nanak (GGS p. 661)

ਗਉੜੀ ਮਹਲਾ ੫

ਗੁਰ ਕਾ ਸਬਦੁ ਰਿਦ ਅੰਤਰਿ ਧਾਰੈ ॥ ਪੰਚ ਜਨਾ ਸਿਉ ਸੰਗੁ ਨਿਵਾਰੈ ॥
ਦਸ ਇੰਦ੍ਰੀ ਕਰਿ ਰਾਖੈ ਵਾਸਿ ॥ ਤਾ ਕੈ ਆਤਮੈ ਹੋਇ ਪਰਗਾਸੁ ॥ ੧ ॥
ਐਸੀ ਦ੍ਰਿੜਤਾ ਤਾ ਕੈ ਹੋਇ ॥ ਜਾ ਕਉ ਦਇਆ ਮਇਆ ਪ੍ਰਭ ਸੋਇ ॥ ੧ ॥
ਰਹਾਉ ॥ ਸਾਜਨੁ ਦੁਸਟੁ ਜਾ ਕੈ ਏਕ ਸਮਾਨੈ ॥ ਜੇਤਾ ਬੋਲਣੁ ਤੇਤਾ ਗਿਆਨੈ ॥
ਜੇਤਾ ਸੁਨਣਾ ਤੇਤਾ ਨਾਮੁ ॥ ਜੇਤਾ ਪੇਖਨੁ ਤੇਤਾ ਧਿਆਨੁ ॥ ੨ ॥
ਸਹਜੇ ਜਾਗਣੁ ਸਹਜੇ ਸੋਇ ॥ ਸਹਜੇ ਹੋਤਾ ਜਾਇ ਸੁ ਹੋਇ ॥
ਸਹਜਿ ਬੈਰਾਗੁ ਸਹਜੇ ਹੀ ਹਸਨਾ ॥ ਸਹਜੇ ਚੂਪ ਸਹਜੇ ਹੀ ਜਪਨਾ ॥ ੩ ॥
ਸਹਜੇ ਭੋਜਨੁ ਸਹਜੇ ਭਾਉ ॥ ਸਹਜੇ ਮਿਟਿਓ ਸਗਲ ਦੁਰਾਉ ॥
ਸਹਜੇ ਹੋਆ ਸਾਧੂ ਸੰਗੁ ॥ ਸਹਜਿ ਮਿਲਿਓ ਪਾਰਬ੍ਰਹਮੁ ਨਿਸੰਗੁ ॥ ੪ ॥
ਸਹਜੇ ਗ੍ਰਿਹ ਮਹਿ ਸਹਜਿ ਉਦਾਸੀ ॥ ਸਹਜੇ ਦਬਿਧਾ ਤਨ ਕੀ ਨਾਸੀ ॥
ਜਾ ਕੈ ਸਹਜਿ ਮਨਿ ਭਇਆ ਅਨੰਦ ॥ ਤਾ ਕਉ ਭੇਟਿਆ ਪਰਮਾਨੰਦ ॥ ੫ ॥

Gur kaa shabad rid antar dhaare. Panch janaa seoo sang nivaarai.
Das indri kar raakhe vaas(i). Taa kai aatmai hooe pargaas(u).
Aisii drirhtaa taa kai hoi. Jaa kau daiaa maiaa Prabh soii.
Rahau. Saajan dusht jaa ke ek samaanai. Jeta bolan tetaa. gianai.
Jetaa sunanaa teta naam(u). Jeta pekhan teta dhiaan.
Sehje jogan sehje soi. Sehje hota jai so hoi.
Sehje beraag sehje hi hasnaa. Sehje choop sehje hii japnaa.
Sehje bhojan sehje bhao. Sehje mitiu sagal da rau.
Sehje hoaa sadhu sang. Sehje maliu parbrahm nisang.
Sehje grah mah(i) sahje udasii. Sahje dab idhaa tan ki naasii.
Ja kai sahaje man bhaiyaa anand. Taa ko bhetia Parmanand.

He who absorbs Guru's word within him, forsakes the five desires.
Controls the ten sense-organs; he is illumined.
He alone has such resolve, on whom His Grace and Mercy is bestowed.
(Pause) Friend and foe seem one to him; wisdom emanates from his mouth.
In whatever he hears, he hears His Nam; in whatsoever he sees he sees Him.
He sleeps in poise and rises in poise; for Him all that happens is accepted in poise.
In poise is he detached; in poise he loves. In poise he is silent; in poise he utters His name.
In poise he eateth; in poise he loveth. All separateness melts for him in poise.
In poise he meets His saints. In poise he feels the Lord's presence.
In poise is he in the household; in poise is he detached. In poise do his doubts depart.
In whose mind exists such joyous equipoise; he is gifted with His presence.

Guru Arjun (GGS p. 236)

A Universal Being

In the Sikh philosophy the self-defeating cycle of joy and sorrow is created by a world view which is self-focused. Such a person is unable to feel joy in other's success, or sorrow in other's tragedies. He celebrates when he gets a promotion and cries when his neighbor gets one.

As a Sikh expands his horizon, he begins to understand that all humans are related to him. He starts to lose the distinction between friend and enemy. He no longer sees his own race or caste as superior to another's. He participates *actively* in this great play, feeling blessed at all times.

ਪ੍ਰਭ ਕੀ ਆਗਿਆ ਆਤਮ ਹਿਤਾਵੈ ॥ ਜੀਵਨ ਮੁਕਤਿ ਸੋਊ ਕਹਾਵੈ ॥
ਤੈਸਾ ਹਰਖੁ ਤੈਸਾ ਉਸੁ ਸੋਗੁ ॥ ਸਦਾ ਅਨੰਦੁ ਤਹ ਨਹੀ ਬਿਓਗੁ ॥
ਤੈਸਾ ਸੁਵਰਨੁ ਤੈਸੀ ਉਸੁ ਮਾਟੀ ॥ ਤੈਸਾ ਅੰਮ੍ਰਿਤੁ ਤੈਸੀ ਬਿਖੁ ਖਾਟੀ ॥
ਤੈਸਾ ਮਾਨੁ ਤੈਸਾ ਅਭਿਮਾਨੁ ॥ ਤੈਸਾ ਰੰਕੁ ਤੈਸਾ ਰਾਜਾਨੁ ॥
ਜੋ ਵਰਤਾਏ ਸਾਈ ਜੁਗਤਿ ॥ ਨਾਨਕ ਓਹੁ ਪੁਰਖੁ ਕਹੀਐ ਜੀਵਨ ਮੁਕਤਿ ॥

Prabh kii aagiyaa aatam hitaavai. Jivan mukat(i) sou kahaavai.
Taisaa harakh taisa oos sog. Sadaa anand teh nahi biyog.
Taisaa suvran, taisi oos maatii. Taisaa amrit taisi bikh khaati.
Taisaa maan taisaa abhimaan. Taisaa rank taisaa rajaan.
Jo vartai saaii jugat(i). Nanak oh purakh kahia jiivan mukat.

He who accepts His will in his heart. Attains deliverance in his life.
As is joy to him, so is sorrow. Always in bliss, never in woe.
As is gold to him, so is dust. As is nectar, so is poison.
As is honor, so is dishonor. As is a king, so is the beggar.
He finds his own path in His will. Nanak, such a person has escaped life's bondage.
Guru Nanak (GGS p. 275)

ਕਰਿ ਕਿਰਪਾ ਦੀਓ ਮੋਹਿ ਨਾਮਾ ਬੰਧਨ ਤੇ ਛੁਟਕਾਏ ॥
ਮਨ ਤੇ ਬਿਸਰਿਓ ਸਗਲੋ ਧੰਧਾ ਗੁਰ ਕੀ ਚਰਨੀ ਲਾਏ ॥ ੧ ॥
ਸਾਧਸੰਗਿ ਚਿੰਤ ਬਿਰਾਨੀ ਛਾਡੀ ॥ ਅਹੰਬੁਧਿ ਮੋਹ ਮਨ ਬਾਸਨ ਦੇ ਕਰਿ ਗਡਹਾ ਗਾਡੀ ॥
॥ ੧ ॥ ਰਹਾਉ ॥ ਨਾ ਕੋ ਮੇਰਾ ਦੁਸਮਨੁ ਰਹਿਆ ਨਾ ਹਮ ਕਿਸ ਕੇ ਬੈਰਾਈ ॥
ਬ੍ਰਹਮੁ ਪਸਾਰੁ ਪਸਾਰਿਓ ਭੀਤਰਿ ਸਤਿਗੁਰ ਤੇ ਸੋਝੀ ਪਾਈ ॥ ੨ ॥
ਸਭੁ ਕੋ ਮੀਤੁ ਹਮ ਆਪਨ ਕੀਨਾ ਹਮ ਸਭਨਾ ਕੇ ਸਾਜਨ ॥
ਦੂਰਿ ਪਰਾਇਓ ਮਨ ਕਾ ਬਿਰਹਾ ਤਾ ਮੇਲੁ ਕੀਓ ਮੇਰੈ ਰਾਜਨ ॥

Kar kirpaa diio mohe Naamaa bandhan te chutkaae.
Man te bisaio sugale dhanda Gur ki charni laae.
Sadhsang chint biraanii chadhii. Ahabhudh moh man baasan de kar gaddha gaddii.
Rohao. Naa ko mera dusman rahiaa naa ham kis ke beraai.
Braham pasaar pasariio bhiitar(i) Satguru te sojhii paaii.
Subh ko miit ham aapan kiinaa ham sabhnaa ke saajan.
Dur paraaio man ka birhaa taa mel kiio merai Rajan.

The Lord has blessed me; my shackles are loosenend.
All involvements have left my mind; I am at my Guru's feet.
The company of saints has melted my cares.
Fathoms deep is buried my ego and attachment.
(Pause) None is now my enemy and I am inimical to none.
Lord has pervaded me. This is the True Guru's wisdom.
I have befriended all; to all I am a friend.
Gone is my separation; I am united with my King.

Guru Arjun (GGS p. 671)

A Happy Warrior

The Sikh is an active participant in life. This often means he has to summon the warrior within him. The Sikh style does not approve of a man who associates overcoming ego with inaction when faced with lifes injustices. Sikh history is filled with events where ordinary men and women rose to face enormous powers to defend themselves and *others*. The greatest martyr in human history, Guru Teg Bahadur, gave his life (beheaded by Emperor Aurangzeb) on behalf of the Hindu Brahmins. *He gave his life for a group of people whose practices and rituals he did not approve.* In fact, the Sikh teachings are in conflict with the lifestyle practiced and proposed by these Brahmins. Yet he was willing to face death to defend the Brahmin's right to practice their religion!

The Sikh warrior is *not the Samurai warrior* in the Japanese culture, willing to face death for his master. He is not the *crusader* in the European culture, pursuing and killing the pagans. Neither is he waging *holy Jihad* to eliminate the infidel. The Sikh warrior is described as a saint-soldier. The saint comes first. The warrior raises his *kirpan* only after he has reached a state of love for all beings — even for his opponents.

ਦੇਹਿ ਸ਼ਿਵਾ ਬਰ ਮੋਹਿ ਇਹੈ ਸ਼ੁਭ ਕਰਮਨ ਤੇ ਕਬਹੂੰ ਨ ਵਰੋਂ ॥
ਨ ਡਰੋਂ ਅਰਿ ਸੋਂ ਜਬ ਜਾਇ ਲਰੋਂ ਨਿਸਚੈ ਕਰ ਆਪਨੀ ਜੀਤ ਕਰੋਂ ॥
ਅਰੁ ਸਿੱਖ ਹੋਂ ਆਪਨੇ ਹੀ ਮਨ ਕੋ ਇਹ ਲਾਲਚ ਹਉ ਗੁਨ ਤਉ ਉਚਰੋਂ ॥
ਜਬ ਆਵ ਕੀ ਅਉਧ ਨਿਦਾਨ ਬਨੈ ਅਤਿ ਹੀ ਰਨ ਮੈ ਤਬ ਜੂਝ ਮਰੋਂ ॥

Deh Shiva bar moh(i) ehai shub karman te kabhun na taran.
Na daron ar son jab jai laron nischai kar apanii jiit karon.
Ar Sikh hon aapnai hi man ko eh lalock hon gun tau ucharon.
Jab aav ki audh nidan bane at(i) hi ran me tab jujh maron.

Grant me this boon, O Lord: I may never be deterred from good deeds.
Without fear I enter the battlefield. With complete resolve I bring victory.
My mind be trained to sing Your praises.
And when my time comes, bring me a valiant death on the battlefield.
Guru Gobind Singh (DG p.99)

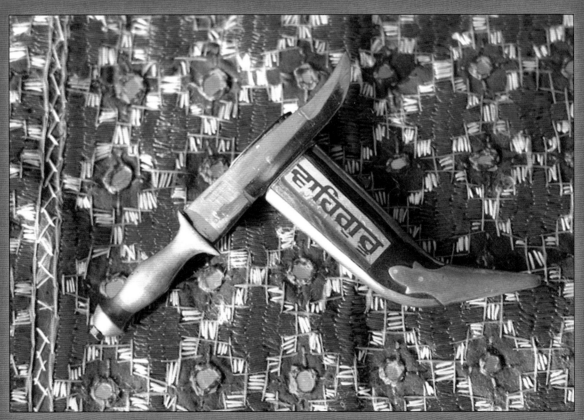

27

The Lion's Symbols

The Sikh style reflects itself in five symbols which the Sikh wears. Many of these symbols have, at times, been a test of the Sikh's resolve. These symbols are not a sign of great wealth or special race or creed. They simply embody the inner style of the Sikh.

KESH: Unshorn Hair

This is perhaps the most distinguishing feature of the outer being of the Sikh. It reflects the style of acceptance of what our Creator has given us. *Kesh* is the most extravagant of the Creator's gift to humans. The Sikh accepts this beautiful gift.

KANGHA: Comb

The *kangha* is a small comb reflecting the action of the Sikh taking great care in keeping his or her *kesh* clean and orderly. The Sikh's *kesh* is not the long hair of the hippie or the dreadlocks of the Hindu *sadhu*.

KACHHA: Shorts

The *kachha* has long been the garment of choice for the sportsman and the men who work with their hands. The *kachha* reflects the respect the Sikh has for physical labor. It also reflects control over the physical senses.

KARHA: Steel Bracelet

The *karha* reflects the resolve a Sikh must have in his life; the resolve to unify his thought and actions.

KIRPAN: Sword

The *kirpan* summons the Sikh to be in touch with his inner warrior. It exhorts him to fight the battles within him and to translate his beliefs into actions, sometimes at great personal risks.

Escaping the Style Master's Web

ਜਿਨਿ ਮਾਇਆ ਦੀਨੀ ਤਿਨਿ ਲਾਈ ਤ੍ਰਿਸਨਾ ॥

Jin Maya Dini Tin Lai Trisna.

He who created Maya also attached in us the craving for it.

Guru Arjun (GGS p.179)

ਹਠੁ ਕਰਿ ਮਰੈ ਨ ਲੇਖੈ ਪਾਵੈ ॥
ਵੇਸ ਕਰੈ ਬਹੁ ਭਸਮ ਲਗਾਵੈ ॥
ਨਾਮੁ ਬਿਸਾਰਿ ਬਹੁਰਿ ਪਛੁਤਾਵੈ ॥

Hath Kar Mare Na Lekhe Pave.
Ves Kare Bah Bhasam Lagave.
Nam Bisar Bahur Pachtave.

Physical deprivations and suffering bring no approval.

Neither does changing robes or application of dust to the limbs.

When the link to Nam is snapped, only grief results.

Guru Nanak (GGS p. 226)

The style of the Sikh is characterized as much by what he or she does *not* do as by what he or she does. As he journeys through life he seeks grace to avoid the sticky web of *maya*. Brilliant minds have been harnessed to weave this web and the most beautiful people have been recruited to spread the word.

Some webs are woven to extract money off of other's insecurities. Enormous markets are created by such web-weavers for tobacco, alcohol, cosmetics, etc. There is little regard for the physical well-being of those trapped. Spiritual web-weavers provide rituals which promise to purge all sins and create an inner bliss. Often these rituals are at best a waste of time, at their worst they can rob one of one's own mind. Social web-weavers create social customs and taboos—many to control and exploit others.

Before examining the Sikh style, let us take a look at some of the webs the great *style masters* of the world have woven. These webs titillate our body, mind and spirit, but for the Sikh, they represent a misguided existence.

In many African countries young girls suffer the humiliating and disgusting ceremony of circumcision. In countries around the world newborn boys are routinely circumcised. As the child leaves the warmth and comfort of the mother's womb, he is greeted with this terrible, painful cut.

The style masters who encourage parents to volunteer their children for these rituals are not any slick Paris or New York advertisement agents — they are religious or tribal leaders. These *branding* rituals give them tremendous control over their *flock*.

ਹਰਿ ਕੇ ਦਾਸ ਸਿਉ ਸਾਕਤ ਨਹੀ ਸੰਗੁ ॥
ਓਹੁ ਬਿਖਈ ਓਸੁ ਰਾਮ ਕੋ ਰੰਗੁ ॥ ੧ ॥ ਰਹਾਉ ॥
ਮਨ ਅਸਵਾਰ ਜੈਸੇ ਤੁਰੀ ਸੀਗਾਰੀ ॥
ਜਿਉ ਕਾਪੁਰਖੁ ਪੁਚਾਰੈ ਨਾਰੀ ॥ ੧ ॥
ਬੈਲ ਕਉ ਨੇਤ੍ਰਾ ਪਾਇ ਦੁਹਾਵੈ ॥
ਗਊ ਚਰਿ ਸਿੰਘ ਪਾਛੈ ਪਾਵੈ ॥ ੨ ॥
ਗਾਡਰ ਲੇ ਕਾਮਧੇਨੁ ਕਰਿ ਪੂਜੀ ॥
ਸਉਦੇ ਕਉ ਧਾਵੈ ਬਿਨੁ ਪੂੰਜੀ ॥ ੩ ॥
ਨਾਨਕ ਰਾਮ ਨਾਮੁ ਜਪਿ ਚੀਤ ॥
ਸਿਮਰਿ ਸੁਆਮੀ ਹਰਿ ਸਾ ਮੀਤ ॥ ੪ ॥ ੯੧ ॥ ੧੬੦ ॥

Har ke das sio sakat nahi sang.
Oh bikkii os Ram ko rung, rahao.
Man aswar jese turi sigari?
Jio kapurukh puchare nari?
Bael ko netra paye duhave?
Gau char singh pachey pavey?
Gaddar le kamdhenu kar poojee?
Saude ko dhavey bin poonjee?
Nanak Ram nam jap cheet.
Simar swami har sa meet.

The Creators servant stays away from the power worshippers.
One is enamored by vice; one by the Lords wonders. (Pause)
Through imagination alone can a man truly ride the decked mare?
Can a eunuch love a woman fair?
Is a bull milked simply by being tethered?
Is a lion pursued by a cows herder?
Can one install a ram as the milk-cow of gods?
Can one with no capital go out to trade?
Nanak, absorb the Lords Name in your mind.
Meditate on Him who is always your friend.

Guru Arjun Dev (GGS p.198)   33

obacco products make up a trillion-plus dollar market. Thousands of people make a great living farming and selling this *legal* drug. Millions other pay for this by getting lung cancer. In the 1940's the tobacco industry recruited Olympic athletes to spread the word on the joy of smoking. The claims were simple — *smoking enhances your physical abilities!* Later, as it became clear that the effect of smoking was in fact exactly opposite, the industry recruited beautiful men and women. The new theme is — *if you smoke you are a non-traditionalist; someone who walks an independent path!*

While the multi-millionaire industrial leaders laugh all the way to the bank, young children around the world light up their cigarettes imagining themselves looking like the rugged cowboy or the adventurous gorgeous lady.

A group which has consistently been manipulated by *male* style masters is the women of this world. From the *burkas* of Afghanistan to the breast implants of the Western countries; from the foot binding of China to the *Sati* of India; from the anti-birth control policies of powerful religions to female infanticide practiced by so many cultures, styles have been developed for women to keep them from controlling their destiny.

In many countries the cultural norms are set by the dominant males. Often the women have little say in the matter. In Western countries the web is woven in such a manner that the woman follows the pre-chosen path all the while thinking that *she is making the decision herself*. What else can explain the fact that over one million otherwise healthy women in the United States alone have had breast implant surgery for no reason other than that the culture has generated an atmosphere where such a practice thrives?

)n a remote seaside resort north of San Francisco, a group of affluent and highly educated men meet. They are all reaching their forties and have spent the last fifteen years of their lives accumulating great success in their chosen careers. Today they are here *to fill the spiritual gaps in their being* as their leader phrases it. They begin filling the gap with a marijuana joint which is passed around the circle. There are mystic sounding drums playing in the background. Soon they share some more potent drinks that make everything look foggy and incredibly lovely. The men are soon hugging each other. Tears of ecstasy are pouring from their eyes. They have found their *Nirvana*. Two days later, bleary-eyed and with hangovers, the men are back at work.

)n a dark alley in Benares in India, a group of holy men gather at the feet of their spiritual master. They are also sharing a joint of *bhang*. Only the surroundings are filthy, far from resort-like. However, the men are all swaying in a sense of bliss!

)t is late at night in a small village. Inside a hall a group of men are swirling at an incredible pace. And they have been doing this non-stop for the last twelve hours! This leads them into a "spiritual bliss."

)t is four in the morning in Benares. At the bank of *Ganga* a man wearing a loincloth is sitting in the lotus position. His face and limbs seem totally out of proportion with his belly. The stomach is so large it seems unreal; as if it were a cartoon drawing. A family is sitting in front of the man and feeding him *laddoos*, each a good four ounces heavy and made from the finest *besan,*[1] sugar and *ghee.*[2] The holy man has already eaten ten *laddoos* and he appears to be just beginning. He eventually eats fifty *laddoos*. The family gives him two one hundred rupee notes which he tucks in his loincloth. This ritual assures the family that not only has the holy man taken over their sins, but has also taken care of their ancestors' spiritual well-being.

   After the family leaves, the holy man goes behind the bushes and rids himself of the *laddoos*, in preparation for his next client.

[1] *Besan is chickpea flour.*
[2] *Ghee is clarified butter.*

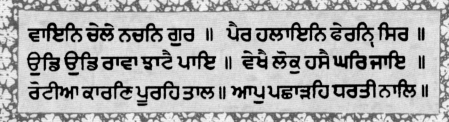

Vayan chele nachan gur. Pair hilain pheran sir.
Ud ud rava jhatai pae. Vekhai lok hasai ghar jae.
Rotia karan pureh tal. Aap pachhareh dharti nal.

The disciples keep the beat, the Guru dances.
He taps his feet, rolls his head.
Dirt is kicked into his hair.
The audience watches, enjoys and returns home.
For a few crumbs of bread is this elaborate dance.
He dashes himself in the ground.

Guru Nanak (GGS p. 465)

Aankhan bheetar tel ko daar, so logan neer bahai dikhaavai.
Jo dhanvaan lakhai nij sewak, tahi paros prashad jimavai.
Jo dhan heen lakhay teh det na, maangan jaat mukho na dikhaavai.
Lootat hai pasoo logan ko, kabahoo na Pramesar kay gun gaavai.

Oil drops in their eyes create a flood of tears to show how they feel other's pain!
A rich disciple is served delicious food.
A poor one begs, but cannot see their faces.
Such beasts loot the masses; little is their connection to God.

Guru Gobind Singh (DG p. 715)

*O*ne of the most extravagant and beautiful gifts our Creator has bestowed upon us is the hair on our faces and heads — *kesh*. *Kesh* occupies a special place in the Sikh religion. We will explore this special status later. But let us see what a non-Sikh has to say on this matter.

Robert Bly, poet and renowned chronicler of men's issues, explores the subject of male hair in his bestseller book *Iron John* (Addison-Wesley, 1990). He identifies four important linkages of kesh to human culture:

- readiness to challenge authority, lack of tameness,
- excess, extravagance, like the extravagance of Mother Earth — forests, wild flowers, rivers, mountains;
- sexual energy and relationship to our animal energy; and
- thoughts, instincts, intuition.

For the Sikhs, kesh also represents an acceptance of our Creator's gift. This acceptance, when carried over to other facets of the Sikh's life, creates the *saint-warrior*. *Kesh* also represents a commitment to the path: "stand up and be counted — sometimes in the face of great risk."

*F*ew other parts of the human body have been more subject to the whims of style masters than *kesh*.

When the communists came to power in China, one of the first things they did was to force all women to get haircuts. According to their philosophy, long hair interfered with the member's duty of hard work and conformity.

In many armies the first thing a new recruit suffers is a head shave — to take away any individuality the person may have. So powerful is the fear of facial hair in the West that it has become a symbol of artists, revolutionaries and even social dropouts, like hippies.

In Nazi Germany, the short-cropped hair style symbolized a character which was unflinching in pursuit of Hitler's mission. Hitler's own haircut and mustache began to symbolize repression and the philosophy of racial superiority. Even now *skin-heads* who view Hitler as a hero sport shaved heads.

Among the Buddhist monks, males and females, a shaved head is essential. To them it symbolizes renunciation. For the Hindu pundits, the head is shaved except for the *bodi*, a little tuft.

The Hindu *sadhu*, on the other hand, leaves his hair alone. The hair is unwashed and uncombed, representing a complete detachment from the world.

igid companies around the world, looking upon their workers as productive robots, impose strict hair cut and hair length rules on them. The worker fearfully obeys.

Robert Bly makes the following observations regarding hair:

"But whether the haired people are symphony conductors with flowing hair, or corporate men with medium-cut, gray flannel hair, so to speak, or the real pruners of extravagance, the fundamentalists who favor crew cuts or shaved heads, the amount of hair allowed suggest how far the instincts are curtailed and the spontaneity curbed."

In Japan, Sumo wrestlers have a special respect. Once they reach yokozuna level, they are allowed the privilege of having long hair. As they age and fall below this level, their hair is chopped off in a special ritual — rendering them just ordinary men!

(Photo from *The Japan Times*, Sunday, February 2, 1992.)

Style of
the Child

Accepting the Gift

The child is a gift of the Creator — not property of the father or mother. In love and warm cuddles it blossoms. The Sikh style rejects any *branding* ceremonies which are widely inflicted upon children. The child is not born in a *sinner* state and there is no need to rescue him by subjecting him to purification rituals. No circumcision awaits him; no dip in *holy* water to jar him; no tattoos to inflict pain upon his little body; no head shavings to purify him.

The Sikh style rejects any mutilation or defacing of the child's beautiful body. The Creator's gift is accepted as is and is nurtured.

The Massage

As a child emerges from the warmth of the womb, he needs touch and complete acceptance. This is the reason massage is so important for the Sikh. Massage provides an important link between parent and child. This link continues well into adulthood.

How wonderful it must feel to a child to lie in warm sun and be massaged with warm oil! What a great trust-creating ritual. Contrast this to the trust-destroying rituals of circumcision, head shavings, or dips in *holy* waters.

Body massages invigorate and exercise the child's limbs while also giving him or her the joy of human touch. As the warm oily hands rub and cuddle the child's arms, legs, chest, back and stomach, the child coos with delight.

As the child grows older, the boys massage is the responsibility of the father. This is a wonderful lifelong ritual. In most cultures, father and son have almost no physical contact. This creates tension between them. Massage allows the father to remain in *touch* with his son. As a massage is given, the father can convey important insights to his son. As the son becomes an adult, he may share this ritual by also giving his father a massage.

The child not only receives regular full body massages; he or she also enjoys head massages. A massage of the head is a central part of the child's physical development. Warm oil is rubbed onto the roots of the hair and the scalp is massaged with a gentle pressure. The massage may last anywhere from fifteen minutes to an hour — the longer, the better!

Hair Care

When the child is a baby, his hair is washed every time he is bathed. As hair grows and is tied, the head bath may occur once or twice per week. Hair must be kept clean and usually is not kept open unless it is being dried. Tying the hair ensures that it doesn't get messy and the child is free to play.

Hair is washed carefully with shampoo or some other home-made concoction (yogurt, *aanwalas*[1], curdled milk...). Once it is thoroughly rinsed, it is dried, preferably in the sun. A hair dryer could be used if the sun is not out and it is cold.

Once the hair is dried, the child has a head massage to look forward to. After the massage, the hair is *brushed very gently* to remove the tangles. The parent must be gentle and patient while doing this.

If the child is very young, say, less than four, his hair can be tied into a small bun by using a hair tie. An elastic hair tie can be used to gather the hair at the base on the top of the head. The hair is then rolled into a bun with a twisting tie. An older child's hair may be braided and tucked at the back of the head.

The *jurha*, a bun tied on the top of the head, is most associated with the way Sikh men tie their hair. The *jurha* is a very versatile style of tying the hair, since it does not loosen even if one is involved in sports. The *jurha* has to be tied by the mother or father until the boy is old enough to do so himself. This usually occurs when he is 12 or 13 years old. Tying the *jurha* is an intimate experience between the boy and the parent. It does not involve any outside barbers or hair stylists — it is a family affair.

In modern life it is not easy for parents to care for children's *kesh* — just as it is difficult to cater to their other physical and emotional needs. It certainly seems more convenient to bring the child to a barber to get his or her *kesh* cropped. But by accepting and nurturing this beautiful gift of the Creator, the Sikh parent also makes a commitment to nurture other facets of the child's life.

[1] *Aanwalas is a kind of herbal shampoo.*

Introduction to Being a Sikh

The Sikh style manifests itself very early in the child's mental and spiritual development. The child learns about the *Gurus* lives and how they made great sacrifices for the causes they believed in. He learns through these stories how a single person of faith can stand against the worlds most powerful forces. He develops faith in knowing that truth and goodness is the path to happiness.

The child will also learn from friends and at school about Hindu, Biblical and other religious stories. He learns about *Ramayan* and *Mahabharat* as well as about the birth of Jesus Christ and Mohammad. He is taught to appreciate the common central themes in all religions. He learns to dissociate myths and legends from the core message.

As the child grows he is taken to the neighborhood Gurdwara where he sees the approach Sikhs take towards fellowship. At home he begins to learn the first *pauri*[1] of the *Guru Granth Sahib*.

[1] *Pauri means stair, i.e., the first few stanzas of the Guru Granth Sahib.*

From Boyhood
to Manhood

From Fantasy to Resolve

How do males make the transition from boyhood to manhood? What is boyhood and what is manhood?

Boyhood is a state where the world of fantasy runs free. The mind floats with the clouds. The boy has muscles that can uproot trees. He has a voice that can make the meanest thug shiver. He can cause the heart of the loveliest maiden to flutter. Boyhood also has its dark sides. His father shouts at him if his grades are poor. The school bully takes away his lunch money. Children laugh and mock his ethnicity. In worse cases, he is abused spiritually, mentally and physically. All of this abuse is transformed into fantasies where he is the hero who saves the world.

Manhood is the state where the male is able to distinguish between fantasy and reality. The man who has reached manhood makes a resolve and keeps it against great odds. How does this transformation occur? Think about this question. How did it occur in your own case?

Manhood does not simply appear with age. Guru Gobind Singhji's *Sahabzadas* were quite young, but Zorawar Singh and Fateh Singh had already reached manhood. How attractive it must have seemed to buckle down, as the wall that eventually bricked them alive was being built around them.

ਮਨ ਅਸਵਾਰ ਜੈਸੇ ਤੁਰੀ ਸੀਗਾਰੀ ॥ ਜਿਉ ਕਾਪੁਰਖੁ ਪੁਚਾਰੈ ਨਾਰੀ ॥ ੧ ॥
ਬੈਲ ਕਉ ਨੇਤ੍ਰਾ ਪਾਇ ਦੁਹਾਵੈ ॥ ਗਉ ਚਰਿ ਸਿੰਘ ਪਾਛੈ ਪਾਵੈ ॥ ੨ ॥
ਗਾਡਰ ਲੇ ਕਾਮਧੇਨੁ ਕਰਿ ਪੂਜੀ ॥ ਸਉਦੇ ਕਉ ਪਾਵੈ ਬਿਨੁ ਪੂੰਜੀ ॥ ੩ ॥
ਨਾਨਕ ਰਾਮ ਨਾਮੁ ਜਪਿ ਚੀਤ ॥ ਸਿਮਰਿ ਸੁਆਮੀ ਹਰਿ ਸਾ ਮੀਤ ॥੪॥੯॥੧੬੦॥

Man aswar jese turi sigari? Jio kapurukh puchare nari?
Bael ko netra paye duhave? Gau char singh pachey pare?
Gaddar le kamdhenu kar poojee? Saude ko pave bin poonjee?
Nanak Ram nam jap cheet. Simar swami har sa meet.

Through imagination alone can a man truly ride the decked mare?
Can a eunuch love a woman fair?
Is a bull milked simply by being tethered?
Is a lion pursued by a cow's herder?
Can one install a ram as the milk-cow of gods?
Can one with no capital go out to trade?
Nanak, absorb the Lord's Name in your mind.
Meditate on Him who is always your friend.

Guru Arjun Dev (GGS p. 198)

Crumbling Resolve

A young boy has few occasions in which to test whether or not he has resolve in his beliefs. He is usually shielded by his parents. He is not subjected to corrupt bosses. He can daydream with little responsibility.

As the boy physically grows he faces the world. He gets a job and soon has to make decisions which test his resolve. Should he be firm in his convictions and lose an important promotion, or should he go along with the unethical practices of his boss and get a hefty pay raise?

When the young man gets married, his fantasy is seriously jarred. His commitment is truly tested. Should he abandon his family and go far away to once again enjoy a carefree life? Or should he hunker down and sacrifice his own pleasures to raise healthy children?

On the social scene, the young man faces new challenges. Practices he had ridiculed as a boy seem quite reasonable and even necessary to him. Should he go out with his buddies and have a drink in the bar or should he go home and spend time with his wife and children? Should he buy an expensive car to impress his neighbors and friends, or should he save the money for some other noble cause?

ਦੂਜੈ ਪਹਰੈ ਰੈਣਿ ਕੈ ਵਣਜਾਰਿਆ ਮਿਤ੍ਰਾ ਭਰਿ ਜੁਆਨੀ ਲਹਰੀ ਦੇਇ ॥
ਬੁਰਾ ਭਲਾ ਨ ਪਛਾਣਈ ਵਣਜਾਰਿਆ ਮਿਤ੍ਰਾ ਮਨੁ ਮਤਾ ਅਹੰਮੇਇ ॥
ਬੁਰਾ ਭਲਾ ਨ ਪਛਾਣੈ ਪ੍ਰਾਣੀ ਆਗੈ ਪੰਥੁ ਕਰਾਰਾ ॥
ਪੂਰਾ ਸਤਿਗੁਰੁ ਕਬਹੂੰ ਨ ਸੇਵਿਆ ਸਿਰਿ ਠਾਢੇ ਜਮ ਜੰਦਾਰਾ ॥
ਧਰਮ ਰਾਇ ਜਬ ਪਕਰਸਿ ਬਵਰੇ ਤਬ ਕਿਆ ਜਬਾਬੁ ਕਰੇਇ ॥
ਕਹੁ ਨਾਨਕ ਦੂਜੈ ਪਹਰੇ ਪ੍ਰਾਣੀ ਭਰਿ ਜੋਬਨੁ ਲਹਰੀ ਦੇਇ ॥ ੨ ॥

Duje pahrai rain ke vanjariaa mitraa bhar juaanii lahrii dai.
Bura bhala na pachhanaii vanjariaa mitraaa man mataa ahanmeii.
Bura bhala na pachhane pranii aage panth kararaa.
Puraa Satguru kabhun na seviaa siri thadde jam jandaaraa.
Dharam raai jab pakrasi bavrai tab kiaa jabab karai.
Kah Nanak dujai pahrai pranii bhar joban lahrii daii.

In the second watch of night, O my merchant-friend,
waves of youth surge within you.
Good and bad you cannot distinguish; your mind is intoxicated with Self.
You distinguished not between good and evil; while the way ahead is arduous.
You served not your True Guru, while the fierce Yama[1] stood overhead.
When Dharamraja seizes you, how then will you respond?
Says Nanak, "In the second watch of night, youth was like surging waves."

Guru Arjun Dev (GGS p. 77)

[1] *Yama is similar to the Grim Reaper.*

The Desire to Flee

Perhaps the most important aspect of manhood is fatherhood. Fatherhood is by far the most important job in the world for a man. However, modern society has created forces that want men to abandon this role. Fatherhood is a great test of a man's resolve to fulfill a commitment. In the U.S.A., the world's richest country, more than half the children are raised today without the presence of a father. The devastation this lack of manhood has caused in the world's richest country is incalculable. Nobody is lamenting this sad state of affairs more than the religious and social leaders of the United States. They realize that the United States of America was built on very solid principles of self-sacrifice and family values. In order to remain the great country that it is, these values must be restored.

Why is it that men who are capable of heading multi-national corporations cannot raise their sons and daughters? Why is it that men who can launch powerful rockets into space, build the fastest computers, become senators in the most powerful nation not be able to hug their sons and be there for them? Because they have not been able to leave the fantasy land of boyhood. Fatherhood is indeed the ultimate test of manhood.

So important is fatherhood that every Sikh Guru who reached adulthood experienced the *fatherhood test*.

Obstacles to Manhood

In the West, numerous books have been written about the deterioration of the father-son relationship and its effect on the inability of boys to become men. Here are some of the reasons they cite:

· The industrial revolution has taken the father to work in some obscure place. The father does things that he often does not agree with and has little control over. He is a small cog in a giant operation. The son never really understands what the father does with his life and, as a result, develops little respect for the father.

"If this is manhood, I don't want it," concludes the son.

· The father, on the one hand, wants to develop as a unique individual and, on the other, wants to look like the *tame and compliant man his company wants.* In his mind he wants to climb mountains, to raise his family at the foothills of a beautiful mountain. In reality, he spends his waking hours trying to make a profit for a faceless corporation. His frustrations and impotence are plain for the son to see.

· The women's movement has given greater power to the man's wife. The mother no longer cowers when the man of the house speaks. She puts him down, often in the presence of the children. And the children remember.

There is ongoing conflict between the husband and wife with often disastrous effects.

· Finally, the sociologists tell us that there is a serious lack of rituals and ceremonies in modern life. One of the most important rituals in the West has become Christmas which is now driven by the battle-cry — *buy, buy, buy!* The lack of rituals and the absence of older men in a child's life have made it extremely difficult for a male to leave the fantasyland of boyhood.

Solutions

What are possible solutions to the problems of fatherless families and men remaining in boyhood? Here are some solutions we can find from the Sikh lifestyle.

• Thriving with Industrialization

It is not possible to simply withdraw from industrial society. There are enormous benefits of industrialization. It is important to realize the connection between the level of financial security people enjoy and industrialization.

However, industrialization also slowly kills the wild and imaginative side of a man. And the man compensates by running from manhood. He is willing to do anything for his boss, but he is unable to comfort a sick child or take him for a hike in the mountains.

How can one live in industrialized society and remain wild and playful? By not allowing the gadgets the industrial world offers to dictate one's life. In other words, by *escaping the web of maya woven by technology.* The three most important webs we face are: i) television, which gobbles up our precious time which should be reserved for the family; ii) an expensive home with expensive gadgets which soak up our earnings, monopolizing our energy as we think of ways to earn more money; iii) rich food and drinks which rob us of physical vitality.

• From Me to Us

Our body is made up of hundreds of mechanisms. Why does one not feel a conflict between the left and right arms? Or between the lungs and the heart? Because the entire body is one unit! In the family there is great conflict because most families are made up of members who have strong *me*-based identities. The benefits of going beyond the *me*-based philosophy is the central theme of the *Guru Granth Sahib*. As the father thinks of the family as himself, he stops abusing the son. As the wife goes from me to us, she stops insulting the father.

• Preserving Sacred Rituals

We all feel pressure to conform to the state demanded by fashion and trend setters. In the mass production market there is enormous money to be made by these people if their version of conformity could be adopted. As a result, they spend millions to make people *go with the flow.* In some cases, they even lobby to pass laws that force people to behave in ways profitable to them. In the process, many traditions that were sacred for centuries are ripped apart. While not all traditions are worth preserving, making profit the sole judge of traditions has had a great price.

Traditions can renew a sense that there is a higher cause — higher than the company. If carried out against opposition, it can be a great character builder.

Does Initiation Into Manhood Require a Wound?

In most old cultures there are important traditions that have been used for centuries to help a boy become a man. Many sociologists have praised the value of these traditions and they have lamented the loss of such traditions from modern societies.

Often, the boyhood to manhood initiation traditions involve a *wound or hurt*. Sociologists say that this is an important part of becoming a man.

In certain societies young boys live essentially with the women until they are ready to be initiated. In an elaborate ceremony, a group of men attack the boy's house and abduct him. They take him to a dark hut where they make him sit in a circle with other men. A knife is produced and each man cuts open a vein and lets some blood into a container. The terrified boy also has to do so. At the end, each person takes a sip. The boy emerges forever transformed.

In other societies an adult circumcision is committed on a boy as he is initiated. In bastardized versions of the boyhood to manhood initiation practiced at many University campuses, young men are made to drink alcohol until they pass out.

In certain regiments young recruits are subjected to terrible humiliation. It is not clear whether the recruits reach manhood. But they do make ruthless killers as a result of these demeaning rituals.

Hath Kar Mare Na Lekhe Pave.
Ves Kare Bah Bhasam Lagave.
Nam Bisar Bahur Pachtave.

Physical deprivations and suffering bring no approval.
Neither does changing robes or application of dust to the limbs.
When the link to Nam is snapped, only grief results.

Guru Nanak (GGS) p. 226)

The Guru's Initiation

Guru Gobind Singh initiated the *Khalsa* through a remarkable ritual. Every Sikh is familiar with the story of when, during the Baisakhi festival, the Guru asked for a volunteer from a large crowd to be beheaded for the Sikh cause. Each time, the Guru took a volunteer into a covered area and emerged with a bloody sword. The five volunteers, or the *panj pyaras*, did not die. The Guru's sword had not gone through their necks, but through a goat's neck. And those few seconds transformed him forever. The ritual also transformed the Sikhs forever!

For the Sikhs, the initiation ceremony from boyhood to manhood does not involve any circumcisions or blood-letting ceremonies. The main initiation is carried out by the Creator Himself.

As a boy reaches the adult age of sixteen to eighteen a remarkable change occurs in his body. The smooth face of the baby is slowly transformed into the face of a man. *This is nature's own initiation into manhood* This is an extremely difficult time for the young man. His entire self-image undergoes a transformation. At one stage the boy has a face like a girl and in a short time hair sprouts from his face!

Why has nature decided to make such a dramatic transformation? Nature is in its own way preparing the male for the task ahead. And the task is enormous. The transformation has to be enormous, too!

In modern societies, with rare exceptions, the response of the family and the son to this transformation is uniformly the same — scrape the hair off the face with blades and razors! Nature's great gift is rejected! The boy does not accept nature's invitation into manhood.

By accepting nature's invitation, the Sikh boy needs no more initiation. If he extends this spirit of acceptance and resolve into other aspects of his life, he has entered manhood. Of course, a Sikh who accepts *kesh* without realizing the significance and without extending this spirit to other aspects of his life remains a boy.

Accepting Face

As nature begins its initiation of boyhood to manhood, powerful forces start aligning to suppress this process. The boy himself does not want to be a man — after all who does not want to continue living in a fantasy? The fashion and razor industries see enormous profits in keeping the boy from accepting his facial hair. The social pundits think that by accepting his newly developing face, the boy may become wild and too individualistic. How will he be controlled?

The forces which work to keep the boy from accepting Nature's initiation also work to prevent a development of other facets of manhood. Enormous money is to be made by the fashion industry from the boy-man. A large chunk of our world economy now depends upon keeping men in a state of infantile fantasy. And often reality has become so painful for men that they are willing to give up everything near and dear to them to remain ensconced in fantasy. Consider this: for more than a decade the United States of America has mobilized its army, border patrol and thousands of drug agents to stop the flow of cocaine and other drugs — with no success. Men willingly squander away their lives for a "hit."

The Sikh accepts his facial hair as part of Nature's gift. The beard, while initially unruly like the lion's mane, soon gives the Sikh's face a dignity and aura. Unlike a shaven face, his face does not feel like sandpaper — smooth from afar, but prickly and grating to the touch. The untrimmed, unshaven facial hair the Sikh accepts is soft to the touch.

Many Sikh men allow the beard to flow unfettered. Contrary to myths propagated by the razor industry, the beard does not grow to be twenty feet long! The beard rarely grows longer than eight to ten inches. Many other Sikhs roll their beards to keep the facial hair more under control. Tying the beard is another intensely personal physical ritual for the Sikh man.

One common style of rolling the beard is to start with a string from under the chin and tied at the top of the head. The beard hair is then carefully rolled around this string. Men in the Indian Armed Forces often tie a beard net (seen at right) once this process is finished.

Here is a method which I like for its simplicity and ease:

· Begin with a slightly moist beard. Massage a very small amount of oil (coconut oil is great) near the roots of the hair.

· With a brush, smoothen the beard. Holding the beard under your chin, make a little ponytail by placing a rubber band around it. I find that rubber bands cut from a bicycle inner-tube work best, since they are quite strong. Each rubber band can last for a week or so before it loses its elasticity. You may need two or three twists of the rubberband to get a good grip on the beard.

· With one finger, open up a little space in the beard just behind the place where the band is gripping the beard's ponytail. Tuck the ponytail into this little space until the entire ponytail is no longer visible.

· Tie a *thhatta* — a piece of cloth about three feet by four inches long, around the beard. Tuck in any loose hair. The beard is tied and in about thirty minutes it will dry. Remove the *thhatta* after thirty to forty minutes. The beard will retain its smooth look for the rest of the day. And it will be soft enough to kiss a baby!

Dastar of
the Sardar

Style for Sale

In the posh boutiques of New York and Paris fashion designers scratch their heads to come up with the next *look* for the "man of style." How should the hair be cut? Should the man with the *look* have sideburns? Should he have a mustache? Should the hair be dyed? Should he wear a cap? Should he don a hat?

The accountants use their laptop computers to churn out the numbers giving the profits to be made if the *look* includes a baseball cap... or if the man could be persuaded to dye his hair... or if he could be coaxed into shaving twice a day, instead of only once.

Once the visionary designers have finalized the *look*, they hire an ad agency to market it. A worldwide blitz is launched. Men with the *look* are shown with women fawning over them; the man with the *look* is successful at everything: business, love, sports, gambling... Men-boys around the world fantasize about the *look* and soon the designer's coffers start to overflow. Success!

The Sikh creates his own style through his *dastar,* or his head-dress. The New York designers are unable to profit from this style. The razor companies are left holding the bag. The Sikh has created his own style. Not even another Sikh can emulate his style — so individual is his *look*.

The Sikh's *dastar* gives him self-confidence and pride. The simplest peasant from the Punjab ties his turban as if he were an Emperor. The *dastar* is the crown of the Sikh. It brings equality between the millionaire and the pauper.

The Beauty of the Pugree

The most beautiful head-dress for men is the hand-tied *pugree* or turban. This head-dress, once banned by the Mughal Emperors for the commoner, identifies the Sikh from near and afar. The Sikh cannot hide in the masses! He must stand and be counted.

The turban or *pugree* is made from fine cotton and usually comes in about one meter width. A visit to a *pugree* shop reveals a multitude of colors. Bright ones for the young at heart! The standard black, maroon, army green, navy blue and steel grey for the mature look! White and saffron for the religious look!

The *simpler* version of the *pugree* involves an approximately five meter long piece of cloth. Men who prefer the fuller *look* may buy eight meters of cloth, cut it in half and make a four-meter-by- two-meter turban to work with.

The Sikh child begins to learn the art of turban tying around his teens. It may take him several years to master the procedure and develop his own personal style to create a work of art.

The *pugree* is sometimes starched lightly, especially if it is to be worn again without re-tying it. Otherwise, one works with the soft, unstarched cloth. The first step is the *punee* where two people stretch the cloth diagonally. The cloth is then folded, while the *pugree* is kept stretched along the diagonal. Both people fold (by rolling) with their right hands, keeping the left side stretched. After the folding, the turban cloth is gathered.

Officers, 35th SIKHS
(Nowgong, India, 1892)

Drill by 14th (Ferozepur) SIKHS
(Rawalpindi, India, 1874)

*B*efore tying the *pugree* the wearer may wrap a colorful *fifty* around his head. The front portion of the *fifty* will be visible on the forehead and adds beauty to the *pugree*.

The tying of the *pugree* is not simple if one wants it to look attractive. Every Sikh boy has spent hours in front of the mirror perfecting the technique. Many Sikh women, particularly American Sikh women, wear beautiful turbans with their distinct styles. One end of the *pugree* is held in the mouth while one gradually wraps the cloth around the head. The angle at which each turn is made, the pinching of the cloth on the forehead, the opening and closing of the folds of the cloth all add subtle touches which lend each *pugree* a unique *look*.

Once the entire cloth is almost used up the last part is tucked in the front taking great care to smooth any wrinkles from this last fold. The end that was clenched in the teeth is now released and pulled to the back of the head. The first fold is now pulled through and opened so that the entire head can be covered. The back end is now pulled back and tucked in.

Tying of the turban is a physical ritual for the Sikh man and for the woman who chooses to wear a turban. It is a ballet, with precise movements of the hands, shoulders and fingers. The cloth is the medium of this art. Once perfected, it only takes a couple of minutes to tie the turban. But it transforms the way the Sikh looks!

A Little Less Formal Style

The Sikh's *dastar* does not always have to be the long turban. Depending upon the situation, Sikhs have developed less formal styles as well. A two meter long piece of cloth (often with an interesting pattern) can make an attractive, less formal *dastar*.

A Lot Less Formal Style

Sikh sportsmen wear the *patka* made from a square piece of cloth (about two feet by two feet) with strings attached on two sides. The *patka* is tied around the head with the *jurha* snugly wrapped in the *patka*'s strings. Often a bandanna can be tied around the head with no strings.

Awakening the Warrior Within

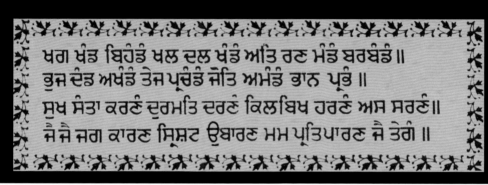

ਖਗ ਖੰਡ ਬਿਹੰਡੰ ਖਲ ਦਲ ਖੰਡੰ ਅਤਿ ਰਣ ਮੰਡੰ ਬਰਬੰਡੰ ॥
ਭੁਜ ਦੰਡ ਅਖੰਡੰ ਤੇਜ ਪ੍ਰਚੰਡੰ ਜੋਤਿ ਅਮੰਡੰ ਭਾਨ ਪ੍ਰਭੰ ॥
ਸੁਖ ਸੰਤਾ ਕਰਣੰ ਦੁਰਮਤਿ ਦਰਣੰ ਕਿਲਬਿਖ ਹਰਣੰ ਅਸ ਸਰਣੰ ॥
ਜੈ ਜੈ ਜਗ ਕਾਰਣ ਸ੍ਰਿਸਟ ਉਬਾਰਣ ਮਮ ਪ੍ਰਿਤਪਾਰਣ ਜੈ ਤੇਗੰ ॥

Khag khand bihandan, khal dal khandan, at run mandan, burbandan.
Bhujdand akhandan, tej prachandan, jot amandan, bhan prabhan.
Sukh santa karnan durmat darnan, kilbikh harnan, us sarnan.
Jai jai jug karan, srisht ubaran, mum pritparan jai teghan.

Lord, as a Sword, you are the conqueror of lands, destroyer of falsehood,
the ultimate decoration of the warrior.
Your arm is indestructable, Your brightness resplendant,
Your radiance and lustre dazzling like the sun.
You bring joy to the saintly, fear to the wicked, the sinners You scatter;
I seek Your shelter.
Hail! Hail! to the Creator, Sustainer of the Universe,
Protector of the creation, Hail to the Sword.

Guru Gobind Singh (DG p. 39)

There was a great warrior named Veer who had acquired a fearsome reputation through his many conquests. Veer's expertise in every possible form of weaponry was sought after by kings and rich lords across the world. However, though he had palaces and servants and his name caused his enemies to shudder with fear, Veer had a deep sense of unease.

One day Veer met a great wise man who seemed to have figured out the secrets of the Universe. Veer spoke, "Master, I have everything a man could want in this life. My friends respect me, my enemies fear me. I am well read and my men are ever ready to die for me. Yet I am deeply unhappy. Give me a task that can bring me bliss in life."

The wise man gave him a strange task. He said, "Go to the bank of the river Dasam. Stick your sword in the sand and meditate beside it everyday for ten hours. When green leaves sprout from the sword, you will find bliss."

Veer was initially suspicious of this strange advice. However, so strongly did he feel his inner unease that he decided to follow the wise man's advice. His men were stunned as he left them. They all felt that he had gone mad.

Months passed as Veer dutifully meditated in front of his sword. Not a sign of greenery appeared on the shining metal. Compared to his previous form, Veer's body was fast becoming frail. He was not exercising and practicing his weaponry.

Almost a year had passed. One morning as Veer prepared for his meditation he heard some cries. Looking up, he saw a chariot approaching. Inside were a woman and her two children. Soon a dozen heavily armed men were upon them. Veer recognized the men as his former fighters. He also recognized the woman to be the wife of an enemy who had wounded Veer in battle many years ago.

To his great surprise, Veer heard himself shout at the fighters to leave the woman and her children alone. The men looked at him with disgust. Their new leader roared back, "Veer, go back to your silly meditation. Look at yourself, you pathetic worm. Your puny arms cannot even lift an ant. Don't say a word to us, otherwise we will chop you up."

His old comrades dragged the woman down and started unloading the chariot's treasures. Meanwhile, somewhat puzzled at himself, Veer leapt to pull out the sword from the sand. In a flash he was upon the leader of the fighters. With a single sweep, his sword pierced the leader's body. Terrified, the remaining men ran off.

Veer turned to comfort his enemy's family. As he turned he saw, from the corner of his eye, green leaves sprouting from his sword. Was it his imagination? He did not turn to verify. Already he was feeling the bliss he had been seeking!

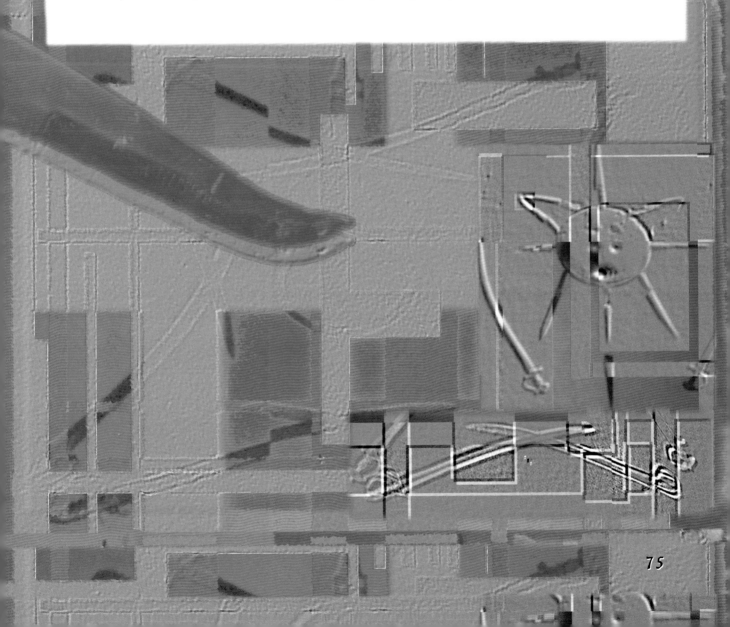

Every small boy has fantasies of slaying giant fire-breathing dragons, subduing hordes of bandits, and saving a few beautiful maidens in the process. In fact, if you observe a young boy daydreaming, most likely he is participating in some great battle!

As the boy grows older, he is confronted with "real life" and slowly abandons his inner warrior. In his job he sees corruption and bribery, but he remains silent, since he likes the security of his job. On the street, he sees thugs selling drugs or insulting a passing woman, but he looks the other way, since he fears he may be beaten up.

As he grows into an older man, he develops a cynical attitude. "Everybody does it," he says as he buys the latest electronic gadget, using money he has received through a bribe. He also manages to subscribe to a highly intellectual philosophy which has taught him to lead a "detached" life. Using some distorted version of "live and let live" he goes about turning a blind eye to life's injustices. He has done a great job of putting his inner warrior to sleep.

The Inner Warrior: Sikh Style

The warrior occupies a central and sacred position in the Sikh philosophy. With the martyrdom of Guru Arjun Dev, the warrior who would stand up and risk all in the fight against injustice started to occupy an increasingly critical role. The tenth Guru formalized the concept of the saint-warrior. Most importantly, the Gurus immersed the Sikh in this remarkable concept with such intensity that it became a practical concept. Acts that were so far only associated with legends and myths became part of history. How remarkable is Guru Teg Bahadur's martyrdom. He willingly gave his life for the cause of Hindu Brahmins. It was not important for him that his own philosophy did not agree with the Brahmins. He was giving his life for human dignity and human rights. Equally remarkable is the fact that even at the young age of twelve and fourteen, Guru Gobind Singh's *sahibzadas* had such a highly developed warrior state. Sikh history is replete with inspiring role-models who were definitely in the class of saint-warriors.

The Warrior

Every successful society has revered its warriors. While religious texts may talk of *Ahinsa*, or "turn the other cheek," in reality armies around the world march with the explicit blessings of priests and other religious leaders. However, the warrior is not always the saint-warrior discussed by Guru Gobind Singh. In the Orient, the exalted warrior was the *samurai* — a highly trained fighter willing to die at a moment's notice for his sworn master. In the West, the crusaders spilled blood to decimate the heathens. Armies have also marched with a desire to bring the *right faith* to the infidels. These are not the saint-warriors the Sikh Gurus refer to. The Sikh response to injustices is not confined to the approaches, "Turn the other cheek;" "An eye for an eye, a tooth for a tooth;" or the often practiced, "An eye for a tooth, a head for an eye." It is the state of the warrior's mind that is of critical importance. Is the state that of a saint?

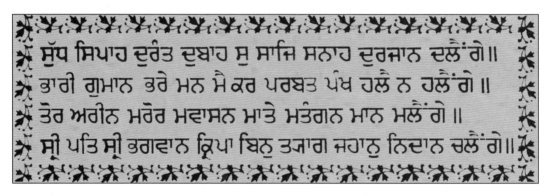

Sudh sipah durant dubah, su saj sanah durjan dalainge
Bhari guman bhare man main, kar parbat pankh hale na haleinge,
Tor arin maror marasan, mate matangan man malainge,
Sri pat sri Bhagwan kripa bin tiag jahan nidan chalainge.

Crack troops, powerful and unconquerable,
in sharp colors and capable of crushing the enemy;
Such pride and ego that mountains may fly away,
but they will not budge from the battlefield;
Tearing up the revolting enemies, twisting their necks,
smashing even the mad elephants;
Yet without His grace, they will meet their worldly end empty handed.

Guru Gobind Singh (DG p. 14)

ਬੀਰ ਅਪਾਰ ਬਡੇ ਬਰਿਆਰ ਅਬਿਚਾਰਹਿ ਸਾਰ ਕੀ ਧਾਰਭਛੱਯਾ ॥
ਤੇਰਤ ਦੇਸ ਮਲਿੰਦ ਮਵਾਸਨ ਮਾਤੇ ਗਜਾਨ ਕੇ ਮਾਨ ਮਲੱਯਾ ॥
ਗਾੜ੍ਹ ਗੜ੍ਹਾਨ ਕੋ ਤੋੜਨ ਹਾਰ ਸੁ ਬਾਤਨ ਹੀ ਚਕ ਚਾਰ ਲਵੱਯਾ ॥
ਸਾਹਿਬ ਸ੍ਰੀ ਸਭ ਕੋ ਸਿਰ ਨਾਇਕ ਜਾਚਕ ਅਨੇਕ ਸੁ ਏਕ ਦਿਵੱਯਾ ॥

Bir apar bade bariar, abichareh sar ki dhar bhachhaya
Torat des malind mavasan, mate gajan ke man malaya
Gare garan ko toran-har, su batan hin chak char lavaya
Sahib Sri Sabh ko sirnaik, jachak anek su ek divaya.

Countless brave soldiers, ever-ready to face the sword's edge;
So many countries conquered, rebels subjugated, wild elephants crushed;
Powerful forts they smash, the world now bows to their mere threat;
Yet God alone is the supreme Commander, at His door they stand as beggars.

Guru Gobind Singh (DG p. 14)

The Saint-Warrior

The saint-warrior looks upon the *kirpan* very much as he looks upon undergoing surgery for a tumor — it is the last resort and it is not because he hates the infected area that he wants removed. *There can be no enimity towards the person the saint-warrior is to combat. The combat is not for a personal gain.*

The saint-soldier has love for entire humanity just as an ordinary man has love for all parts of his body. Just as no sane person will cut off his left arm so that the right one may become stronger, the saint-soldier will not lift his sword for the benefit of a king or a landlord, or even for his own benefit.

ਦੇਹਿ ਸ਼ਿਵਾ ਬਰ ਮੋਹਿ ਇਹੈ ਸ਼ੁਭ ਕਰਮਨ ਤੇ ਕਬਹੂੰ ਨ ਵਰੋਂ ॥
ਨ ਡਰੋਂ ਅਰਿ ਸੋਂ ਜਬ ਜਾਇ ਲਰੋਂ ਨਿਸਚੈ ਕਰ ਆਪਨੀ ਜੀਤ ਕਰੋਂ ॥
ਅਰੁ ਸਿਖ ਹੋਂ ਆਪਨੇਹੀ ਮਨ ਕੋ ਇਹ ਲਾਲਚ ਹਉ ਗੁਨ ਤਉ ਉਚਰੋਂ ॥
ਜਬ ਆਵ ਕੀ ਅਉਧ ਨਿਦਾਨ ਬਨੈ ਅਤਿ ਹੀ ਰਨ ਮੈ ਤਬ ਜੂਝ ਮਰੋਂ ॥

Deh Shiva bar moh(i) ehai shub karman te kabhun na taran.
Na daron ar son jab jai laron nischai kar apanii jiit karon.
Ar Sikh hon aapnai hi man ko eh lalock hon gun tau ucharon.
Jab aav ki audh nidan bane at(i) hi ran me tab jujh maron.

Grant me this boon, O Lord: I may never be deterred from good deeds.
Without fear I enter the battlefield. With complete resolve I bring victory.
My mind be trained to sing Your praises.
And when my time comes, bring me a valiant death on the battlefield.
Guru Gobind Singh (DG p.99)

ਨਾ ਕੋ ਮੇਰਾ ਦੁਸਮਨੁ ਰਹਿਆ ਨਾ ਹਮ ਕਿਸ ਕੇ ਬੈਰਾਈ ॥

Naa ko mera dusman rahiaa naa ham kis ke beraai.

None is now my enemy and I am inimical to none.
Guru Arjun (GGO p. 671) **81**

Preparation of the Saint-Soldier

The first ingredient in the saint-soldier is the saint. The saint within us must be first cultivated before one can think of using the *kirpan*. It is the saint who allows a person to develop a universal outlook. The saint has no enemy; all humanity is made up of his bosom buddies! Once a man or woman reaches this level, he or she will have no difficulty identifying when cancer has developed in the human mass. When all non-violent action fails, the warrior is nudged to take action.

ਕਹਾ ਭਯੋ ਦੋਊ ਲੋਚਨ ਮੂੰਦਕੈ ਬੈਠਿ ਰਹਿਓ ਬਕ ਧਿਆਨ ਲਗਾਇਓ ॥
ਨ੍ਹਾਤ ਫਿਰਿਓ ਲੀਏ ਸਾਤ ਸਮੁੰਦਨ ਲੋਕ ਗਇਓ ਪਰਲੋਕ ਗਵਾਇਓ ॥
ਬਾਸ ਕੀਓ ਬਿਖਿਆਨ ਸੋ ਬੈਠ ਕੈ ਐਸੇ ਹੀ ਐਸ ਸੁ ਬੈਸ ਬਿਤਾਇਓ ॥
ਸਾਚੁਕਹੋ ਸੁਨ ਲੇਹੁ ਸਭੈ ਜਿਨ ਪ੍ਰੇਮ ਕੀਓ ਤਿਨ ਹੀ ਪ੍ਰਭੁ ਪਾਇਓ॥੯॥੨੯॥

Kaha bhayo jo dou lochan mund kai, baith rahio bak dhian lagaeo,
Nhat phirio lie sat samundran lok gayo parlok gavaio,
Bas kio bikhian so baith kai, aise hi aise su bais bitaio,
Sach kahon sun leh sabhai jin prem kio tin hi Prabh paio.

Why sit with closed eyes pretending like a crane to be in deep meditation?
Bathing (in holy waters) and traveling the seven seas (in pilgrimages),
losing both this world and the next one as well,
Seated they waste their time in useless discussions,
Here is the truth for all to hear, only through love is He realized.

Guru Gobind Singh (DG p. 14)

Preparation of the Warrior

With the best of intentions a warrior cannot take a worthwhile action if he is not mentally and physically fit. A man carrying too much *excess baggage* cannot survive in combat. The excess baggage may be a large belly cultivated through a lifestyle of fatty foods and drinks. It may be a comfortable lifestyle based on ill-gotten money.

How can a man who can barely run a hundred yards challenge an opponent?

How can a man whose chief aim in life is to make money take a stand against injustice?

ਰੇ ਮਨੁ ਐਸੋ ਕਰਿ ਸੰਨਿਆਸਾ ॥
ਬਨ ਸੇ ਸਦਨ ਸਭੈ ਕਰਿ ਸਮਝਹੁ ਮਨ ਹੀ ਮਾਹਿ ਉਦਾਸਾ ॥
ਰਹਾਉ ॥ ਜਤ ਕੀ ਜਟਾ ਜੋਗ ਕੋ ਮੱਜਨੁ ਨੇਮ ਕੇ ਨਖਨ ਬਢਾਓ ॥
ਗਿਆਨ ਗੁਰੂ ਆਤਮ ਉਪਦੇਸ਼ਹੁ ਨਾਮ ਬਿਭੂਤ ਲਗਾਓ ॥
ਅਲਪ ਅਹਾਰ ਸੁਲਪ ਸੀ ਨਿੰਦ੍ਰਾ ਦਯਾ ਛਿਮਾ ਤਨ ਪ੍ਰੀਤਿ ॥
ਸੀਲ ਸੰਤੋਖ ਸਦਾ ਨਿਰਬਾਹਿਬੋ ਹੁਵੈਬੋ ਤ੍ਰਿਗੁਣ ਅਤੀਤਿ ॥
ਕਾਮ ਕ੍ਰੋਧ ਹੰਕਾਰ ਲੋਭ ਹਠ ਮੋਹ ਨ ਮਨ ਸੋ ਲਯਾਵੈ ॥
ਤਬ ਹੀ ਆਤਮ ਤਤ ਕੋ ਦਰਸੇ ਪਰਮ ਪੁਰਖ ਕੌ ਪਾਵੈ ॥

Ray man aiso kar sanyaasaa
Bun say sadan sabhai kar sajhah man hi maah udaasa
Jat ki jattaa jog ko majjan men key nakhan rahao
Gain Guru aatam upadesh naam bibhoot lagaao
Alap ahaar sulap si nindraa dayaa chhimaa tan preet
Seel santokh sadaa nirbaahbo huwaibo trigun ateet,
Kaam krodh hankaar lobh hathh moh na man sou lyaray
Tab hi aatam tat ko darsay param purakh kah pavai.

O man loosen your shackles thus,
Treat your home as a forest retreat and have the heart of a hermit,
Make continence your matted hair, communion with God your ritual bath
and righteous living your ritual long nails.
Make divine knowledge your center and smear your body with ashes of God's name.
Eat little and sleep little; love the practice of compassion and forbearance.
Be calm and contented and you will be in control of three states
(desire; ignorance and laziness; good living).
Keep lust, anger, pride, greed, obstinacy and worldly attachments at bay.
Thus will you see your own essence and reach the highest level.

Guru Gobind Singh (DG p. 709) **85**

Physical Fitness: A Test

The Sikh style strives to develop a human who is physically, mentally and spiritually fit. The easiest aspect of this universal style is physical fitness.

While it is difficult to test how fit one is in the spiritual realm or even in the mental world, it is not so tough to test oneself in the physical world. Of course, a visit to the doctor can give us an idea of our medical condition. But armies around the world have developed tests to check the fitness of the elite soldiers. Here is one such test. Perform it after checking with your doctor, and if you have never exercised regularly, spend at least six months working out before taking this test.

This is a typical test for entering the elite corps of most of the world's armies. It tests stamina and strength.

- 2 mile run: less than 15 minutes
- 60 push-ups: less than 2 minutes
- 20 pull-ups: less than 2 minutes

The push-ups and pull-ups must be done in good form.

Test By Fire:
Family Life

ਸਚਹੁ ਓਰੈ ਸਭੁ ਕੋ ਉਪਰਿ ਸਚੁ ਆਚਾਰੁ ॥

Sach ure, Sabh ko uchai sach aachaar.

Truth is the highest virtue, higher still is true living.
Guru Nanak (GGS p. 62)

*A*s humanity welcomes the dawn of the twenty-first century, the world's only superpower finds itself with an unfortunate malady. Half of all marriages in the United States end in divorce. Religious and social leaders in the West are appalled at this breakdown of the family and are fighting hard to help rebuild it. After all, the great Western culture was built on a very strong sense of family and social responsibilities. Even the liberal sociologists who until recently held the view that divorce has minimal impact on the future generation now are rethinking the effects of this social rot. In this rich and resourceful country it is estimated that three-fourths of adult men have no regular contact with children. Other developed countries of the West are not far behind. And even traditionally highly family-oriented developing countries are beginning to see the initial stages of this disease develop.

Indeed the most difficult battles faced by men of today's societies are not the high-tech nuclear and biological battles, but the battle within their homes. And like the cold-war, these battles also have only losers. The man may be able to put on a powerful facade for the outside world, but finds his children ripping off his mask and puncturing his parachute.

Men who have won against incredible odds in the battlefield, who have built giant businesses, who have penned inspiring books, who have reached pinnacles in the arts and sciences, find themselves running scared from their own families. The thought of hugging their own sons is so terrifying to some men that entire psychological therapies have been developed to overcome this fear and resultant guilt.

The household is indeed the ultimate test by fire of manhood.

All of the Sikh Gurus who reached marriageable age got married and raised families. They witnessed the ups and downs of family life first-hand. This is in contrast to most philosophers and founders of many religions who either had no children, no relations with a woman or may have abandoned their families in search of "truth." How could such men present a positive view of family life in general and of women in particular? The Sikh religion firmly believes that there is complete compatibility between a householder's life and a high spiritual life. In fact the Sikh Gurus were quite critical of men who tortured their bodies by denying it its physical needs and took to the forest in search of *nirvana*.

Family life cannot be blissful if the man looks upon his wife and children as his property. If so he will fret if his wife uses her own mind. Or if his children question his decisions. For a blissful life, the man has to abandon his *I know best* attitude and look at his family as a gift from the Almighty. A gift to be nurtured.

Family in Jeopardy

What is the cause of such widespread breakdown of families in the developed countries? Experts point to two key reasons:

(i) The growing independence (social and economic) of women and the inability of men to reconcile to their new status;

(ii) An economic system that has brought the concepts of capitalism (concepts that have provided such abundance for humanity in most cases) right into the family-life decisions. When family decisions are based on maximizing financial profit, the "unproductive" children (and sometimes non-income-earning wife) become liabilities. And it becomes financially seductive to abandon the liabilities.

The woman is also subjected to the same seduction as the man and may often opt for the path of least resistance. And sometimes this may mean self over family. However, due to the mother's biologically different role in the family, it is less likely that the mother will abandon the children. Nevertheless, the web that encourages self-gratification snares both men and women.

ਰਾਜ ਮਹਿ ਰਾਜੁ ਜੋਗ ਮਹਿ ਜੋਗੀ ॥   ਤਪ ਮਹਿ ਤਪੀਸਰੁ ਗ੍ਰਿਹਸਤ ਮਹਿ ਭੋਗੀ ॥
ਧਿਆਇ ਧਿਆਇ ਭਗਤਹ ਸੁਖੁ ਪਾਇਆ॥ ਨਾਨਕ ਤਿਸੁ ਪੁਰਖ ਕਾ ਕਿਨੈ ਅੰਤੁ ਨ ਪਾਇਆ ॥

Raj mahi raj jog mohi jogii. Tap mehi tapisar, grahst mahi bhogi.
Dhiai dhiai bhagtah sukh paiyaa. Nanak tis purakh ka kinai ant na paiaa.

He is King among kings, Yogi among yogis.
An ascetic among ascetics, indulgent in the household.
Through His meditation devotees find peace.
Nanak, for that person no limits exist.

Woman's Status

In nearly every society the woman has been treated as a second class citizen. Elaborate myths and legends have been developed by men to degrade and vilify the woman. In Western religions the woman is supposedly the cause of the fall from grace for man. In the great Indian mythology of *Mahabharat* the heroes of the legend, the *Pandavas*, lost their wife Draupadi in a card game! She was offered after their other valuables, like gold and land, had been lost in the gambling game.

When the wife is treated as the property of the man, there is no possibility of a joyous family life. The husband who strikes his wife, or abuses her emotionally, or insults her by having a mistress is failing himself and his family. In the past, when women had few recourses, such a family could remain intact, although at great emotional cost to all living in it. But with the emerging power and self-confidence of women such families are doomed.

ਭੰਡਿ ਜੰਮੀਐ ਭੰਡਿ ਨਿੰਮੀਐ ਭੰਡਿ ਮੰਗਣੁ ਵੀਆਹੁ ॥

ਭੰਡਹੁ ਹੋਵੈ ਦੋਸਤੀ ਭੰਡਹੁ ਚਲੈ ਰਾਹੁ ॥ ਭੰਡੁ ਮੁਆ ਭੰਡੁ ਭਾਲੀਐ ਭੰਡਿ ਹੋਵੈ ਬੰਧਾਨੁ ॥

ਸੋ ਕਿਉ ਮੰਦਾ ਆਖੀਐ ਜਿਤੁ ਜੰਮਹਿ ਰਾਜਾਨ ॥

ਭੰਡਹੁ ਹੀ ਭੰਡੁ ਉਪਜੈ ਭੰਡੈ ਬਾਝੁ ਨ ਕੋਇ ॥ ਨਾਨਕ ਭੰਡੈ ਬਾਹਰਾ ਏਕੋ ਸਚਾ ਸੋਇ ॥

ਜਿਤੁ ਮੁਖਿ ਸਦਾ ਸਾਲਾਹੀਐ ਭਾਗਾ ਰਤੀ ਚਾਰਿ ॥

ਨਾਨਕ ਤੇ ਮੁਖ ਉਜਲੇ ਤੀਤੁ ਸਚੈ ਦਰਬਾਰਿ ॥

Bhand janmiai bhand ninmiai bhand mangan viah.
Bhandoh hovai dostii bhandoh chalai rah.
Bhand muaa bhand bhalia bhand hovai bandhaan.
So kio mandaa aakhai jit janmeh rajaan.
Bhandoh hi bhand uupjai bhandai baajh na koe.
Nanak bhandai baahra eko sacha soe.
Jit mukh sada saalaahia bhaga rati chaar.
Nanak te mukh ujle tiit sachai darbar.

Nourished in her womb, born of her, he is betrothed and married to a woman.
With her you get friendship and through her does civilization originate.
When she dies you seek another for through her does the household continue.
Why call her low from whom kings are born?
From one woman is another born; none can be born without her.
(Guru) Nanak says only God has originated without her.
That face is fortunate and as beautiful as a jewel which praises Him.
Such a face will be bright in God's court.

Guru Nanak (GGS p. 473)   **93**

From Me-Based to Us-Based

One of the central messages of the *Guru Granth Sahib* is the need to control *hau-maii* or the me-based life. Nowhere is this need greater than in ensuring a happy family life. As our lives become more intertwined with the interests of global market forces and international conglomerates, the need for an us-based value system is critical if the family is to remain intact and happy. And without a strong family the next generation of humanity will be lost.

A distinguished economics professor[1] at the Massachusetts Institute of Technology recently conducted a study to document the economic benefits to a man who abandons his family! While the professor was making a point that purely economics driven decisions are incompatible with intact families and was by no means advocating divorce, his study sheds important light on what happens when me-based value systems pervade our lives.

If indeed the man in the family (usually the higher earner) places his own welfare above that of his children and wife, he quickly comes to the conclusions which the MIT professor found. The first conclusion is that children are *profit sinks* and deplete the family of wealth (counted in dollars). If the man continues his thinking along these lines and takes a path consistent with this thinking, he sees no room for children in his life. If however, he has already had children, he sees a great value in divorcing the family. This motivation is strengthened since his mindset has also ensured that he has very poor relations with his children.

It is clear that if men are to prove the MIT professor's verdict incorrect, they have to replace their me-based decisions with us-based decisions. It may be more attractive for the me-based man to go to a bar with his buddies, but for the us-based man it would appear more enjoyable to play with his son. It may be more pleasing for the me-based man to watch four hours of sports on the television, but for the us-based man, a visit to a park with his family would seem more pleasurable.

[1] Professor Lester C. Thurow.

> ਜਾ ਕਉ ਚਿੰਤਾ ਬਹੁਤੁ ਬਹੁਤੁ ਦੇਹੀ ਵਿਆਪੈ ਰੋਗੁ ॥
> ਗ੍ਰਿਸਤਿ ਕੁਟੰਬਿ ਪਲੇਟਿਆ ਕਦੇ ਹਰਖੁ ਕਦੇ ਸੋਗ ॥
> ਗਉਨੁ ਕਰੇ ਚਹੁ ਕੁੰਟ ਕਾ ਘੜੀ ਨ ਬੈਸਣੁ ਸੋਇ ॥
> ਚਿਤਿ ਆਵੈ ਓਸੁ ਪਾਰਬ੍ਰਹਮੁ ਤਨੁ ਮਨੁ ਸੀਤਲੁ ਹੋਇ ॥

Ja ko chinta bahut bahut dehi viyape rog.
Grast kutamb paletiya kade harakh kade sog.
Gawan kare chah kant ka gharhi na baisan soye.
Chik ay ave os parbraham tan man sital hove.

If one's mind is saturated with worries, the body is ravaged with disease.

Household responsibilities have engulfed; now there is joy, now sorrow.

Four continents are traveled, but not a spot to rest.

Let the Creator into the heart; mind and body are at peace.

Guru Arjan Dev (GGS p. 70)

Style
Within
Society

If one were to identity a single feature that best describes the Sikh social style, it would have to be the *langar* — the Sikh communal meal. The *langar* is a meal prepared by Sikhs in their homes or in their *Gurdwaras* to be shared by Sikhs and non-Sikhs, by rich and poor, by the so-called high class and the not-so-fortunate. It is not a meal of charity where only the destitute of the society come. It is an honor for every Sikh regardless of his or her position in life to sit and share a meal with his fellow men and women. While the *langar* is served daily in most *Gurdwaras*, on Guru Nanak's birthday, Sikh families across the world get together to prepare this simple meal. Strangers and friends gather in an open common courtyard to share this meal.

The *langar* symbolizes the Sikh social style through: (i) *seva*, or volunteerism; (ii) a disregard for the taboos of castes, creed and skin color; and (iii) caring for the community at large regardless of the individual's religious background.

For the Sikhs, *langar* is a part of life. For non-Sikhs who have participated in a *langar*, it leaves a lasting impression. Once when I was at a busy corner of Ginza in Tokyo, a man came to me to ask directions. He was from Thailand and was a visitor in Japan. After I helped him to the best of my ability, I asked him why he had asked me— an obvious visitor in the country. He said, "because you are a Sikh. Once when I was in Thailand, I was really down on my luck. I didn't even have money for food. A friend of mine told me to go to a *Gurdwara*. I had *langar* there for a whole week. You people have a very big heart!"

When the Sikh Gurus initiated the practice of *langar*, it was unthinkable for a high caste man to sit by a low-caste man; for a rich man to sit on the floor and share a meal with a poor man; or for a Muslim to even eat from the same utensils that were used by a Hindu. Six hundred years later as we reach a new millennium, the importance of people from different religions, of different castes and races sitting and sharing a simple meal is still a rarity only seen at a *langar* on a regular basis.

Equality of Human-kind

The *Guru Granth Sahib* has, in addition to the teachings of the Sikh Gurus, passages from Hindu and Muslim saints of the time. The most important social message to the Sikh is to believe in the equality of human-kind. There is no room in this philosophy for superior races or superior skin colors. There is no inherent superiority in men over women, or vice-versa. There are no chosen people of God based on birth. This concept is extremely difficult to bring into practice. Humans, by nature, derive pleasure from degrading another human. Elaborate social structures are set up to put a fellow human down through barriers of caste, color, wealth, and even religion. Social *pundits* have defended such barriers. They have predicted that if these barriers are removed, society will fall into a deep abyss. The reality is that the fall of these barriers will only destroy such *pundit's* parasitic livelihood.

There is indeed a pleasure to be derived from beliefs in a superior race, color or tribal affiliation. There is also great pleasure in slandering and mocking others not in one's social *compartment*. But these pleasures are similar to the pleasure resulting from eating one's own flesh! The delicious taste one feels in the mouth is at the expense of an invalid body.

ਮਿਥਿਆ ਸ੍ਵਣ ਪਰ ਨਿੰਦਾ ਸਨਹਿ ॥ ਮਿਥਿਆ ਹਸਤ ਪਰ ਦਰਬ ਕਉ ਹਿਰਹਿ ॥
ਮਿਥਿਆ ਨੇਤ੍ਰ ਪੇਖਤ ਪਰ ਤ੍ਰਿਅ ਰੁਪਾਦ ॥ ਮਿਥਿਆ ਰਸਨਾ ਭੋਜਨ ਅਨ ਸ੍ਵਾਦ ॥

Mithia sravan par ninda sunah.
Mithia hasat par darab kau harah.
Mithia netra pekhat par tria ruupaad.
Mithia rasnaa bhojan an svaad.

False are the ears that hear slander.
False the hands that snatch what is another's.
False the eyes that see another's bride.
False the tongue that tastes not Him.
Guru Arjun (GGS p. 268)

100

Seva — Volunteerism

    The Sikh religion advocates a lifestyle wherein the aim of life is not to reach the forest and abandon all ties to society, but to reach a balanced life in the thick of society. *Seva* is an important ingredient of this lifestyle. In *seva* an individual works for others or for a common cause without expecting to be compensated in any material way. The work itself is the compensation. Those who volunteer know this joy.

ਪੰਜਿ ਨਿਵਾਜਾ ਵਖਤ ਪੰਜਿ ਪੰਜਾ ਪੰਜੇ ਨਾਉ ॥
ਪਹਿਲਾ ਸਚੁ ਹਲਾਲ ਦੁਇ ਤੀਜਾ ਖੈਰ ਖੁਦਾਇ ॥
ਚਉਥੀ ਨੀਅਤਿ ਰਾਸਿ ਮਨੁ ਪੰਜਵੀ ਸਿਫਤਿ ਸਨਾਇ ॥
ਕਰਣੀ ਕਲਮਾ ਆਖਿ ਕੈ ਤਾ ਮੁਸਲਮਾਨੁ ਸਦਾਇ ॥
ਨਾਨਕ ਜੇਤੇ ਕੂੜਿਆਰ ਕੂੜੈ ਕੂੜੀ ਪਾਇ ॥

Panj nivajaa vakhat panj panjaa panje nau
Pahilaa sach halal dui tijaa khair khudai
Chauthi niiat raasi man panjvii sifat sanaai
Karni kalmaa aakh kai taa musalmaan sadaai
Nanak jete kurhiaar kuurhai kuurhi paai.

Thou sayest thy prayers five times, giving them five names;
Let Truth be the first, honest living the second, good of all the third;
Fourth prayer be honest mind, the fifth, praise of the Creator;
Any other prayer is false; False is their value.
Guru Nanak (GGS p. 141)

Stand Up and Be Counted

We have already discussed the importance of awakening the inner warrior. The saint-warrior must participate in society as a guard against exploitation by the powerful. As societies evolve, the causes for which one must stand up and be counted also change. However, the courage and resolve needed for these new causes still requires men and women with resolve and ability to distinguish causes that are important for all people — not just for one's own self-centered interests. This is possible if one is able to break from the web of *Maya*.

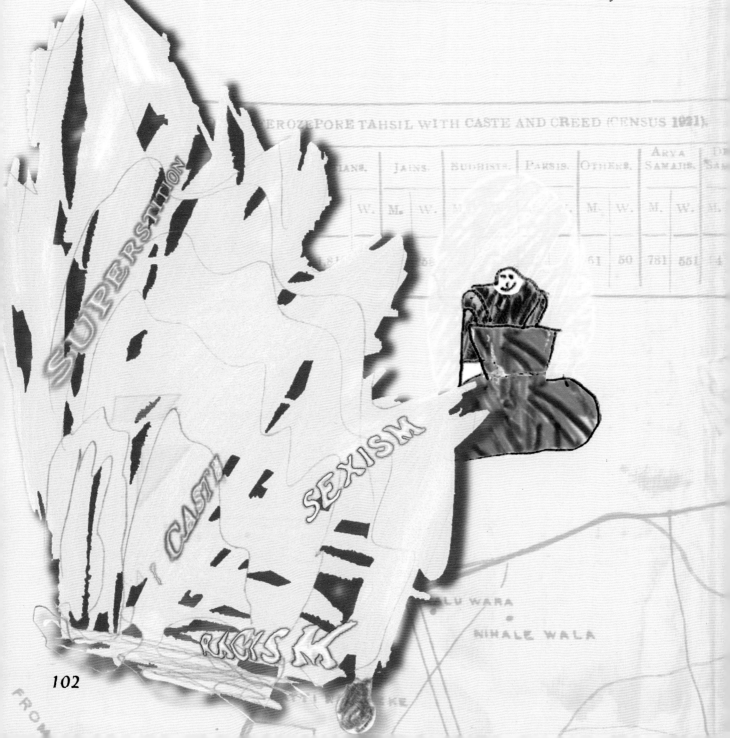

ਵਡੇ ਵਡੇ ਰਾਜਨ ਅਰੁ ਭੂਮਨ ਤਾ ਕੀ ਤ੍ਰਿਸਨ ਨ ਬੂਝੀ ॥
ਲਪਟਿ ਰਹੇ ਮਾਇਆ ਰੰਗ ਮਾਤੇ ਲੋਚਨ ਕਛੂ ਨ ਸੂਝੀ ॥੧॥
ਬਿਖਿਆ ਮਹਿ ਕਿਨ ਹੀ ਤ੍ਰਿਪਤਿ ਨ ਪਾਈ ॥
ਜਿਉ ਪਾਵਕੁ ਈਧਨਿ ਨਹੀ ਧ੍ਰਾਪੈ ਬਿਨੁ ਹਰਿ ਕਹਾ ਅਘਾਈ ॥ ਰਹਾਉ ॥
ਦਿਨ ਦਿਨ ਕਰਤ ਭੋਜਨ ਬਹੁ ਬਿੰਜਨ ਤਾ ਕੀ ਮਿਟੈ ਨ ਭੂਖਾ ॥
ਉਦਮੁ ਕਰੈ ਸੁਆਨ ਕੀ ਨਿਆਈ ਚਾਰੇ ਕੁੰਟਾ ਘੋਖਾ ॥

Vaddai vaddai rajan ar bhuman taa kii trisan naa buujhi
Lapat rahai maya rang maatai lochan kachuu naa suujhi
Bikhia mahi kin hii tripat naa paaii
juou paavak iidhani nahii dhraapai bin har kaha aghaii (rahao)
Din din karat bhojan bahu binjan taa ki mitai naa bhukhaa.
Uddam kare suaan kii niaaii chaarai kantaa ghokha.

Great kings and landlords could not quench their cravings;
Engulfed in maya, their eyes saw not the true Path;
None could satiate his thirst of desire;
As fire is not satiated by firewood; who can be content without Him?
Though like a dog one runs now for this, now for that in all directions.

Guru Arjun (GGS p. 672)

Facing Life's Odds

ਡਰੀਐ ਜੇ ਡਰੁ ਹੋਵੈ ਹੋਰੁ ॥
ਡਰਿ ਡਰਿ ਡਰਨਾ ਮਨ ਕਾ ਸੋਰੁ ॥

Dariye je dar hove hor.
Dar dar darna man ka sor.

Why be afraid when there is no other fear.
And all other fears are but noises in the mind.

Guru Nanak (GGS p. 151)

Rare is the human being who during the course of his life has not had to travel through life's darkness. Darkness where all seems to be lost. Where there seems to be no hope or way out. And perhaps men who have never gone through such a period through their entire lives have not received the final finish. They remain soft and insecure. Just as an athlete cannot reach his potential without putting his body through grueling work-outs, a man cannot reach his true stature without battling the demons that life's tragedies bring forth.

It is through the dark times that a man's faith is tested. Will he be able to retain his balance or will he falter? In this vulnerable state man becomes anxious to grasp at meaningless rituals. He is willing to believe in cults that ask him to hand over his life to them They will run his life and during this dark time it seems like the best choice to some. Charlatans and quacks emerge from every corner to strip him of his dignity and to enrich themselves through his tragic state.

But it is also in this dark state that a man can test his beliefs and theories. He can test his spiritual and physical muscles.

ਬਲੁ ਛੁਟਕਿਓ ਬੰਧਨ ਪਰੇ ਕਛੂ ਨ ਹੋਤ ਉਪਾਇ ॥
ਕਹੁ ਨਾਨਕ ਅਬ ਓਟ ਹਰਿ ਗਜ ਜਿਉ ਹੋਹੁ ਸਹਾਇ ॥੫੩॥
ਬਲੁ ਹੋਆ ਬੰਧਨ ਛੁਟੇ ਸਭੁ ਕਿਛੁ ਹੋਤ ਉਪਾਇ ॥
ਨਾਨਕ ਸਭੁ ਕਿਛੁ ਤੁਮਰੈ ਹਾਥ ਮੈ ਤੁਮ ਹੀ ਹੋਤ ਸਹਾਇ ॥੫੪॥

Bal chhutkayo bandhan pare kachu na hot upae.
Kah Nanak ab oat har gaj jayo hoye sahae.
Bal hoya bandhan chute sabh kich hot upae.
Nanak sabh kich tumare hath me tum hi hot sahae.

My strength has dissipated, shackles enclose me, there seems no escape.
Says Nanak: You are my shelter; empower me as you have your saints.
My strength has returned: my shackles are shattered; all doors are open.
Says Nanak: all is in Your hands; I lean on You.

Guru Teg Bahadur (GGS p. 1429)

105

Triggers of Darkness

Darkness can be triggered into a person's life through a number of events.

· A highly developed inner warrior may force one to take a stand against incredible odds. This may result in great personal harm. The body may be maimed, loved ones may be lost. Sikh history is replete with such stands against seemingly impossible odds. Guru Gobind Singh promised the *Khalsa*: "I will make the sparrow fight the hawk!"

· Situations beyond one's control may cause grave illnesses and rob one of vitality. "Why me?" is the natural response.

· Mighty men of this world may decide to make life a living hell. Giant faceless corporations may make arbitrary rules and cause layoffs or unbearable work conditions.

· Drugs or alcohol may take one into life's abyss. It may seem impossible to break the addiction.

· People who were loved and trusted may decide for apparently no reason to betray one. It may send one into despair.

Attitude is Everything

The spiritual and mental attitude with which one faces life's dark periods is the key to how one emerges on the other side. The self-pitying *"why me?"* attitude opens the key to the door which leads down the path where charlatans and quacks can rob one's dignity. The *"why not me?"* attitude allows one to emerge strengthened. The tragedy has been viewed as a challenge and the individual and society is better off once the clouds pass.

ਜਾ ਕੈ ਦੁਖੁ ਸੁਖੁ ਸਮ ਕਰਿ ਜਾਪੈ ॥ ਤਾ ਕਉ ਕਾੜਾ ਕਹਾ ਬਿਆਪੈ ॥੧॥
ਸਹਜ ਅਨੰਦ ਹਰਿ ਸਾਧੂ ਮਾਹਿ ॥ ਆਗਿਆਕਾਰੀ ਹਰਿ ਹਰਿ ਰਾਇ ॥੧॥

Ja ke dukh sukh sam kar jape.
Ta ko karha kahan biyape.
Sahaj anand har sadhu mahe.
Agiyakari har har rai.

When pleasure and pain look alike,
How can sorrow touch one.
The saint resides in eternal bliss.
For he/she understands the Creator's work.

Guru Arjun Dev (GGS p. 186)

Since tragedies and life's uncertainties are bound to strike sooner or later, how does the Sikh prepare for them? Here is what the Guru advises us.

· As you lose your self-centered style and develop a more universal style, personal ups and downs seem less thrilling and frightening. The ability to take joy in another's joy and feel another's sorrow provides the *balance* needed to face life's individual darkness.

· The faith that nature's laws are constant — in the physical and spiritual world — is essential in preventing missteps in darkness. Charlatans will love to *fix the stars* or put in a *personal good word to God for you* — for a small price. Sometimes the price is money, sometimes it may involve handing over the control of your mind to them.

It is critical for the Sikh not to fall into the trap of tricksters and cult leaders in times of darkness.

· Look at life as the great play run by *Waheguru* in which joyful parts and tragic parts are all to be played as a challenge. One does not puff up when good fortune smiles and get deflated at the slightest prick.

· Turn difficult challenges into resources for humanity. Throughout history men and women have overcome great challenges and used them to leave gifts for humanity. New medical treatments have been endured by people with grave illnesses to provide cures to others. Brave men have suffered the torture of being skinned alive to ensure that future generations can practice their religions in dignity.

Kahu lai pahan puj dhario sir, kahu lai ling gare latkaio.
Kahu lakhio har(i) avachi disa hah(i), kahu Pachhah ko sis(u) nivaio.
Kou butan ko pujat hai pas(u), kou mritan ko pujan dhaio.
Kur kriya urjhio sabh hi jag, Sri Bhagwan ko bhed(u) na paio.

There are some who worship stones held on their heads;
some who carry stone idols around their necks.
Some describe God as residing in the south; some prostate to the west.
Gripped in false ceremonies is this world; true wonders of the Creator lost.

Guru Gobind Singh (DG, p. 14) **107**

Enterprise and Unbounded Optimism

A belief system that incorporates universal brotherhood and sisterhood of humanity, one that rejects degrading rituals, caste systems and racial superiority, and one that strives to achieve bliss through action, is not only good for the spirit — it also generates thriving communities.

The Sikh is spread across all corners of the world. He has not gone to these corners as a conqueror or to convert the native — he has gone with a sense of adventure and enterprise and with a belief that this great world is for all to share. Everywhere the Sikh has gone, he has thrived. There have been occasional acts of discrimination, but the Sikh does not dwell on them. His motto is always the same: *Thriving, not surviving!*

Thanks to Yogi Harbhajan Singh, many Westerners have been exposed to the beauty of the Sikh style. The Westerners who have accepted this faith bring to it their unique energy and spirit. Often, Sikhs who have been born into Sikhism are impressed by the beauty and grace of these "new" Sikhs.

The Sikh has not thrived because he is intrinsically more brilliant than others. Nor because he has unusual physical attributes. The reason is perhaps this: *he is unfettered by superstitions and his actions are unencumbered by "I-know-God-better"-priests and astrologers.* He has no problems breaking bread with the so-called *low-castes* or the heathens or *kafirs.* He does not wait for auspicious alignments of stars to make life decisions. And most importantly, the Sikh does not accept poverty and suffering as a necessity for a high spiritual life. On the contrary, he associates physical deprivation with silliness.

The Sikh style of enterprise has often come into conflict with the political climate of the times. The most recent example of this has resulted in the massacre of thousands of Sikhs in 1984. The now-repudiated Soviet inspired fiscal policies of the Indian government created financial deprivation which was particularly unacceptable for Sikhs. This, and not any inherent Hindu-Sikh conflict, caused the disastrous event which led to the 1984 tragedy.

The adage *kirit karo, vand chakho, Nam japo* – put forth the enterprise, share the labor's fruit and keep your life in accordance with *Nam* – guides the Sikh and ensures physically, mentally and spiritually healthy individuals and societies.

In the following pages, glimpses of some Sikhs are presented. Some of these men have accomplished enormous deeds and are well-known. Others may not have such widespread fame, but are nevertheless heroes in their own special ways. They embody the spirit of *"charhdi kala"* — unbounded optimism. This is not a catalogue of *Who's Who* of Sikhs. Such a catalogue would take volumes. The following pages simply present a glimpse of the Sikh spirit.

Piara Singh Data

At eighty-seven, Piara Singh Data is an inspiring personality. His decades of mountaineering and hiking have kept his body lean and with a straight posture. Author of over fifty books, his intellect is sharp. An active participant of the Indian freedom struggle as a young man, Sardar Piara Singh has been a poet, a writer of short stories and novels and a press owner for most of his life. His love and contributions to the Punjabi language has made him a living treasure.

Hari Pal Singh Ahluwalia

I asked Hari Pal Singh Ahluwalia the question, "How are your typical days?" His answer: "My days are bright. Everyday is full of brightness."

Major Sahib (as he is known) climbed the world's highest peak, Mt. Everest, in 1965 becoming an instant celebrity in India and abroad. His handsome face graced the covers of numerous newspapers and magazines. Through incredible training and determination he had overcome one of the most daunting challenges. However, a much greater challenge lay ahead.

During the Indo-Pakistan war of 1965, while defending the supply lines to Ladhakh, HPS was hit by a bullet which left him a paraplegic. At that time there was no treatment center for spinal injuries in India. With indomitable courage and persistence he underwent his own therapy (mostly outside India) while pursuing a seemingly impossible task — to build and run a world class spinal injury center in India. Three decades of hard work together with his infectious optimism has resulted in the realization of this dream.

Most of us will neither climb the Everest nor be confined to a wheelchair. But all of us can draw strength from this incredible man.

General Jagjit Singh Aurora

After a most delightful interview with Gen. Aurora ended, he walked us to our car parked outside his home. Several men in uniform snapped to salute him. From afar the general spied our driver, Pargat, and hailed him with the greeting, *"Kee haal hai bhai?"* (How are you, brother?). In a culture where hierarchies and status pervade the atmosphere, what a refreshing attitude! To me this greeting sums up the General's down-to-earth style.

For most people around the world General Aurora is associated with the history-making event of the birth of a Nation — Bangladesh. He was the military leader and the brain behind the blitzkrieg that in thirteen days caused the surrender of the powerful Pakistan army in 1971. However, Jagjit Singh had many more exciting and momentous tasks in front of him after this achievement.

After retiring from the army, the General worked as a high power executive in Calcutta, a parliamentarian and a great statesman. His statesmanship was especially important during and after the 1984 anti-Sikh riots in India. He set up two tasks for himself. The first involved helping with the education of the children and finding work for the widows. The second was to bring the perpetrators (many of whom were police officers and government officials) to justice. In his own words, "We were quite successful with the first task. The generosity and hard work of the Sikhs was again reflected. We were not so successful in the second task. Even after twelve years we are waiting. However, a very important turn around has occurred in regard to the public's image of the Sikhs. There is a complete reversal of anti-Sikh sentiment. As a result, even though the guilty are not in jail, they are suffering a worse fate."

Nineteen-eighty four had been a test of the Sikh enterprise and spirit. General Aurora was an important calming force at that time. While there was irreparable loss of human life, the Sikhs and the Indian nation has used this tragedy to better itself. Sikh owned businesses that were burned to the ground are now flourishing. India itself is becoming a more truly open market where human potential is less harnessed by bureaucracy and fear. In 1997 around New Delhi are giant posters announcing the ban on smoking in all public buildings. Three decades earlier when Sikhs made such a demand for the environs of the Golden Temple, the country ridiculed them!

Man Mohan Singh Kohli

When Sardar Man Mohan Singh Kohli started recalling for me the number of professions he had in his life (so far!), I was truly amazed. Let us see — a navy officer, perhaps the most outstanding Everest expedition leader, promoter of tourism in the Himalayan ranges, banker in Hong Kong, the man who brought the Outward Bound program to India, hotel owner...

Man Mohan is most famous for his remarkable mountaineering exploits. Under his leadership, nine men conquered the world's highest peak. He himself spent three days in the *death zone* — the 28,000 foot point from where the final ascent to the peak is made — two of them without oxygen!

His zest for life caused him to take a leadership role in numerous mountaineering programs — both national and international in scope. His work in the area of conservation projects for the Himalayas are recognized around the world.

At the young age of sixty-five, Man Mohan is running his own Inn in Delhi — a world-class place with a climbing wall in the lobby!

"I've been thinking about your project," Kohli told me, "I think the special style of the Sikhs comes from the fact that they do not have the concept of impossible in their intellect."

Surrinder Singh Nakai

Brigadier Surrinder Singh Nakai (now retired from Rajputana Rifles) was among the first group of Indian army personnel to undergo nuclear and biological training in the USSR. "My turban and beard opened doors all across Russia. Whether it was receiving tickets to the Bolshoi or receiving the company of the fair sex on the dance floor!"

On a more serious note, this striking man feels that the Sikhs need to carry out research to keep the *kesh* compatible with modern technologies as used in warfare or on the playground.

Mewa Singh Sangha

In Sardar Mewa Singh's face you see the character of a man of the soil — solid and able to absorb anything life throws at him. Nobody suffers through life's ups and downs like a farmer. And no other profession gives a greater sense of individuality and accomplishment. The Sikh farmer has always provided the Sikh society at large the vigor and fortitude for which it is known. The farmer cannot live in a fantasy world; he learns to face his tasks — everyday.

As Mewa Singh inspects his near-ripe crops, he feels the joy of performing a task — from start to finish.

Epilogue

In this book we have tried to give the reader a glimpse of the spiritual, mental, physical and social style of the Sikh. Let us end with a short story from the life of Guru Nanak which captures his view of the Creator.

During one of his travels, Guru Nanak came upon some learned priests offering gifts to the glory of the Creator. Each priest had offered his own precious gift. Guru Nanak, however, stood by calmly. He was asked, "Do you not have something to offer to your Creator? A coconut, some milk, perhaps some precious stone? What kind of worship do you believe in?" In his response Guru Nanak uttered one of the most beautiful compositions, part of which is reproduced on the following page.

As humanity grapples with our serious environmental problems where the beautiful earth is threatened through greed or ignorance, it is affirming to meditate on this hymn composed five hundred years ago.

ਧਨਾਸਰੀ ਮਹਲਾ ੧ ਆਰਤੀ

ੴ ਸਤਿਗੁਰ ਪ੍ਰਸਾਦਿ ॥ ਗਗਨ ਮੈ ਥਾਲੁ ਰਵਿ ਚੰਦੁ ਦੀਪਕ ਬਨੇ ਤਾਰਿਕਾ ਮੰਡਲ ਜਨਕ ਮੋਤੀ ॥
ਧੂਪੁ ਮਲਆਨਲੋ ਪਵਣੁ ਚਵਰੋ ਕਰੇ ਸਗਲ ਬਨਰਾਇ ਫੂਲੰਤ ਜੋਤੀ ॥ ੧ ॥
ਕੈਸੀ ਆਰਤੀ ਹੋਇ ਭਵ ਖੰਡਨਾ ਤੇਰੀ ਆਰਤੀ ॥ ਅਨਹਤਾ ਸਬਦ ਵਾਜੰਤ ਭੇਰੀ ॥ ੧ ॥ ਰਹਾਉ
ਸਹਸ ਤਵ ਨੈਨ ਨਨ ਨੈਨ ਹੇ ਤੋਹਿ ਕਉ ਸਹਸ ਮੂਰਤਿ ਨਨਾ ਏਕ ਤੋਹੀ ॥
ਸਹਸ ਪਦ ਬਿਮਲ ਨਨ ਏਕ ਪਦ ਗੰਧ ਬਿਨੁ ਸਹਸ ਤਵ ਗੰਧ ਇਵ ਚਲਤ ਮੋਹੀ ॥
ਸਭ ਮਹਿ ਜੋਤਿ ਜੋਤਿ ਹੈ ਸੋਇ ॥ ਤਿਸ ਕੈ ਚਾਨਣਿ ਸਭ ਮਹਿ ਚਾਨਣੁ ਹੋਇ ॥ ਗੁਰ ਸਾਖੀ ਜੋਤਿ ਪਰਗਟੁ ਹੋਇ ॥
ਜੋ ਤਿਸੁ ਭਾਵੈ ਸੁ ਆਰਤੀ ਹੋਇ ॥ ੩ ॥ ਹਰਿ ਚਰਣ ਕਮਲ ਮਕਰੰਦ ਲੋਭਿਤ ਮਨੋ ਅਨਦਿਨੋ ਮੋਹਿ ਆਹੀ ਪਿਆਸਾ ॥
ਕ੍ਰਿਪਾ ਜਲੁ ਦੇਹਿ ਨਾਨਕ ਸਾਰਿੰਗ ਕਉ ਹੋਇ ਜਾ ਤੇ ਤੇਰੈ ਨਾਮਿ ਵਾਸਾ ॥

Gagan main thaal Rav chand deepak bane tarika mandal janak moti;
Dhup malaanlo pavan chavro kare sagal banrai phulat jotii.
Kaisii aaratii hoi bhav khandnaa teri aarati.
Anhata sabad vajant bherii. Rahao.
Sahas tav nain nan nain hai tohi kau, sahas murat nana ek tohi.
Sahas pad bimal nan ek pad gandh bin sahas tav gandh iv chalat mohii.
Sabh mahi jot jot hai soi. Tis ke channan sabh mai channan hoi.
Gur sakhii jot pargat hoi. Jo tis bhave su aarati hoi.
Har charan kamal makrand lobhit mano andino mohi aahi piyasaa.
Kirpa jal dehi Nanak maring kau hoi jaa te terai Nam vasaa.

With sky the salver, the sun and the moon the lamps,
galaxies of stars studded as jewels;
With chandan scented winds from the Malai mountains fanning,
myriad flowers illuminating the spectacle;
Thus is your worship performed, O Destroyer of fear, this is your worship.
The melody rings and music of the Word is made as if on a tender flute. (Pause).
Thousands are Thine eyes, yet hast thou eyes?
Thousands thy form, yet hast Thou a form?
Thousands are Thy lotus-feet, yet hast Thou feet?
Thousands Thine noses, yet hast Thou a nose?
Thou art the Spirit that flows through all. Your light illumines all.
Through the True Guru's wisdom Your light appears...
What pleases Thee becomes Thy worship.
(Like the honey bee) all day I crave the honey of Thine lotus-feet.
Bestow upon Nanak the nectar of Thy grace, so he can merge in Thy Name.

Guru Nanak (GGS p. 663)

118

For this and other hi-quality books and
publications on Sikh Heritage, please contact:

THE
SIKH FOUNDATION

580 College Ave., Palo Alto, CA 94306, USA
Phone: (650) 494-7454
Fax: (650) 494-3316
sales@sikhfoundation.org
info@sikhfoundation.org
www.sikhfoundation.org